Schiffer Publishing

Library of Congress Control Number: 2019934841



Edited by Ian Robertson
Designed by Matt Dipalma
Cover design by Jack Chappell
Type set in Boca Raton/ DIN/ Bembo/ Berliner Grotesk

ISBN: 978-0-7643-5863-0
Printed in China

Published by Schiffer Publishing, Ltd.
4880 Lower Valley Road
Atglen, PA 19310
Phone: (610) 593-1777; Fax: (610) 593-2002
E-mail: Info@schifferbooks.com
Web: www.schifferbooks.com

**To Mole and Glen,**

without whose friendship I would never have made it this far.

Thank you, Gentlemen!

# Table of Contents

From the late 1800s and found at an antique mall, this photo illustrates that men and women trading clothing for each other's amusement is not new in photographic history. As Dr. Bohleke points out, "it is one heck of a cross-dressed scene." *Courtesy of Dr. Karin Bohleke*

# Foreword

Nineteenth-century photographs regularly show comic gender role reversal through the medium of clothing exchange. Quite often—particularly in group images—the trade entailed switching hats and bonnets, as well as capes and coats, illustrating that they were most likely a spontaneous decision under circumstances where a full exchange of garments was not possible due to the surroundings, setting aside the question of fitting a man into a corset and a tight bodice. From this point of view, the *soldatinnen* that form the basis of this publication belonged to a well-established comic tradition among friends of which they would have been quite aware.

In the context of impending and current warfare, the image of a woman in a loved one's uniform—whether it be that of a husband, brother, father, or fiancé—acquires additional layers of meaning. For Western societies in the 1930s and 1940s, separate spheres of responsibility for each gender still held significant sway. When their soldiers left for the front, these women had to be and indeed were willing to step into their jack boots—figuratively speaking—and function quite literally as the "man" of the house. Viewed from this perspective, the cross-dressed portraits of ladies in a *soldat*'s uniform represent the women's visual and symbolic acceptance of their added responsibilities in connection with the war effort and managing the home front. It also implies their support of the men's departure and of the war itself, as well as their equality with men in rising to the occasion and being willing to make the ultimate sacrifice for their ideals.

Virginia Woolf famously connected war and clothing in her essay *Three Guineas* (1938), which is widely available online in e-book format. She argued that for men, "your finest clothes are those you wear as soldiers," and added that the "splendor" of the formal dress uniform was designed to "impress the beholder with the majesty of the military office," as well as "through their vanity to induce young men to become soldiers." The spectacle of the marching ranks and files of proud men, designed to forge support for the group identity, also most likely encouraged women to allow their menfolk to leave in the first place. In Woolf's opinion, women had no other real choice in the society in which they operated, as a result of a patriarchal order at the time that denied women universal education, professional opportunities, and a real chance to voice dissent or alternative courses of action. In other words, the *soldatinnen* pictured here had no other choices before them.

Woolf committed suicide in March 1941 and so did not live to see the slow and grim progress of combat, which did not end until 1945. At the onset of the war Germany was already incapable of providing for civilian needs, and the situation continued to deteriorate through the emphasis on military production, chronic shortages, Resistance sabotage, and Allied bombing campaigns. As the Nazi downfall approached, women wore the uniforms again, only without lighthearted comedy among friends and loved ones. With the creativity born of desperate need, they donned the men's trousers—both uniform and civilian—and held them to their waists with strings or curtain cords. By this time, the Nazi Party had no choice but to relax its strictures against women wearing pants in public, since it had to confront the far larger issue of overwhelming defeat. The women also picked up jackets abandoned by retreating German soldiers, restyled Hitler Youth uniforms, and overdyed other military jackets. They also secretly turned swastika flags into garments. But most tragic of all, having little left to wear, a number of them wore their husbands' military jackets. They embroidered, trimmed, and otherwise patched the holes left by the bullets that took the men's lives. The uniforms were no longer "the finest clothes," and the men were dead. The women were now well and truly the head of the household, stepping into the men's figurative shoes when they were very nearly barefoot.

For those interested in learning more about the role of fashion, politics, gender ideology, and clothing production during the Third Reich, I highly recommend Irene Guenther's book *Nazi Chic? Fashioning the Woman in the Third*

*Reich* (Oxford: Berg, 2004). The book reconstitutes the tension between the worlds of fashion and survival that formed a significant part of each woman's wartime story and serves to remind all that, with some historical exceptions, wars are never really over in a just few short months as propaganda and enthusiasm anticipate.

Collections such as this take years to compile, and it is a fitting tribute to the women that Matthew DiPalma has done just that, preserving in this way a defining moment in their life story.

Dr. Karin J. Bohleke
*Director, Fashion Archives & Museum*
*Shippensburg University*

# Acknowledgments

A love of history does not occur overnight, and when others who share that same passion inspire one to delve deeper, that joy of learning and discovery becomes all the more special. I cannot thank all of my fellow reenactors enough for being there to share their fascination of history, the hobby, and one another's heartfelt company. Thank you to those who have inspired me, especially the late Donald Bowman, who shall remain in my heart as a true friend and one of the most inspiring examples of a gentlemen I have ever known. Thank you also to those reenactors who have looked to me to be *their* inspiration, for giving me the opportunity to be a part of their impressions and for sharing in their love for historical interpretation.

Apart from collecting ephemera, my wife and I have gathered a number of original nineteenth- and twentieth-century photographs for our clothing research. Had it not been for Phillip and Janine Whiteman of PNJW Collections, it would have taken so many more years to realize how valuable such items could be in that quest, and so I would like to thank them both for being an inspiration, genuine scholars, and true friends. They have always been eager and willing to share their knowledge and their collections with us and have been a shining example of how two people who do it right can be as valuable as any museum.

Special thanks, too, to Cherri Picard and my wife, Penny, for their assistance in dating a number of the pre–World War I images. Avid historical interpreters and clothing aficionados, Cherri and Penny have a wealth of knowledge of period clothing styles, which helped me establish a number of dates for the majority of images in chapter 1, all while sharing their humor, their appreciation of history, and their wonder over the images we evaluated.

I owe a great deal of thanks to historical interpreters who researched and represent the development of early photography in their portrayals and services at reenactments, particularly Fritz Kirsch, Wendell Decker, and Claude Levet. Their use of original cameras and materials, and the painstaking blend of chemicals and processes, has been an unending source of fascination for me, not to mention their attention to detail and skill at photography.

Mostly, I would like to thank Dr. Karin Bohleke, not only for her foreword, but for the feedback and additional direction she provided. The questions she raised sent me digging in what turned out to be marvelous research about film development and gender reversal in wartime Germany. Her queries allowed me to strengthen and enhance this work beyond my original intent and will, I hope, allow readers to view the details of photos within their own collections with a finer eye.

Thank you to everyone who contributed to making this book a reality!

# Introduction

It is not often that one can point to a photograph and immediately recognize the country and era that produced it. Civilian portraiture tends to blend from one nation and time period to the next because, in the course of just a few short years, so little distinguishes one from the other. For example, European portraits from the latter half of the nineteenth century are very similar because of the similarity in culture, clothing, hairstyles, and so forth; one must often rely on the markings and language on the reverse before a clear identification can be made.

A young woman wearing a Wehrmacht *Waffenrock* and *Tuchhosen* stands outside a home, posing for her photographer.

Yet there is one form of civilian portraiture that stands out as uniquely identifiable in both time and place to the first half of the twentieth century. During the First World War, studio photographers of France, Germany, and the Austro-Hungarian Empire capitalized on patriotic fervor and the vigor of youthful men. Eventually, this kind of photography became a personal passion of German soldiers in the war that followed.

What emerged from this trend? Snapshots and personal photographs of wives, mothers, sisters, and girlfriends of the almost eighteen million soldiers, airmen, and sailors of the Third Reich, which remain widely available and reasonably priced for the avid collector of militaria, photography, and portraits.

*Soldaten* took the majority of these candid photos while on leave, evidenced by the badges and medals on the uniforms earned on campaign. Most are lighthearted and humorous mementos of happier times for homesick soldiers far from home and missing their loved ones. Some depict the soldier and his loved one swapping apparel; women wear the soldier's uniform, while their men wear that of their loved one: a dress, a ladies' coat, or even a ladies' uniform, such as that of a nurse, complete with her white nurse's cap.

This subgenre is not unique to Nazi Germany, though with the exception of France, few personal snapshots of women wearing their husbands' uniforms exist from other nations. Photos of women in their own uniforms are common, but those of women in men's uniforms are far more rare.

This work does not concentrate on uniforms worn by women who served in various official functions of the Reich, such as the Reichsbahn, or the Postal Service, or the numerous roles filled by women in the Wehrmacht. In fact, I focus primarily on the humorous cross-dressing of wives and family for their own amusement, or for the entertainment of their *soldaten*.

These are snapshots taken by amateurs, not professional photographers; a number of images are off-center, soft focused or out of focus, light leaked, and frequently over- or underexposed. This adds an air of authenticity, in that it proves that these were common family portraits by everyday soldiers, airmen, and sailors. It exposes (no pun intended) the average *soldat* for what

One of the earliest suppliers of commercially available cameras and photographic supplies, Voigtländer Foto celebrated their 100th year in this original advertisement from 1943. When Voigtländer initially opened their doors, photography was just a little over five years old.

he was: a human being, prone to the same mistakes and foibles as everyone else, photographic or otherwise.

As with my previous work, I have maintained period conventions when referring to the names of German military organizations. For example, the term *Wehrmacht* refers to the German armed forces of the Third Reich, not just the army. The army was referred to as *das Heer,* the air force as *die Luftwaffe,* and the navy as *die Kriegsmarine.*

I have kept translations true to their original intent and not necessarily literally word for word, except in instances where such might allow additional understanding of the phrase. Each phrase or word will be translated, either parenthetically or in the body of the text; I have also provided a glossary in the appendix. As in other works, I have opted to spell German words that use "ß" as "ss," per the recently adopted convention, not because I am new to German (I've been speaking it on and off since 1973), but because many English speakers tend to confuse it with the letter "B."

Figure numbers are noted in the captions, the first number of which indicates the chapter; for example, figure 2-15 refers to the fifteenth figure in chapter 2. Many of the images have been reduced or enlarged to fit the format of this book and, when possible, to increase visibility of the details; original sizes have been noted in the captions.

As one may imagine, this book is not meant to be an all-inclusive attempt to identify every single photograph taken of women in their husbands' or boyfriends' uniforms during the Third Reich. Rather, it is a representational overview of the kinds of pictures German soldiers and their families found amusing, as well as an informative guide to the overwhelming number of original photos available to collectors and enthusiasts today.

Readers are welcome to send me any comments they may have; I would be more than happy to receive any insights or corrections for future editions.

Figures 1-1 through 1-8. When many people think of old photographs, they think of the ferrotype, better known as the tintype. A cheap imitation of finer photography of the day, the tintype outlasted its predecessors, remaining a full century after its introduction. Tintypes were often trimmed to fit within paper sleeves or photo albums, such as the commercially available sleeves in the figures at the bottom. (shown at approximately 65% of original size)

# 1

# A History of Portraiture in Photography

To understand what makes photography such an interesting aspect of portraiture as a genre, one must understand how and why portrait photography became so popular. By this I do not mean studio portraits, but rather, the candid and amateur personal snapshots so prominent during the twentieth century, the small photos before the advent of digital photography, and how the quest to capture a permanent image on paper led to it all.

## The Birth of Photography

The history of photography goes back much further than one would expect, back to antiquity and the discovery of the camera obscura in China and ancient Greece at roughly the same time (fourth century BCE). The Latin name coined by Johannes Kepler at the beginning of the seventeenth century refers to how the phenomenon was best viewed; one started with a room that is considerably darker than outside (a *camera* is a large open room and *obscura* is Latin for dark, also written as *oscura*). A small hole not much larger than a peephole in a door was often the primary source of light into the room. As the light entered, it cast an inverted image of the outside world against the opposite wall.

This optical trick does not rely solely on darkened rooms; Aristotle noted that the weave of a basket, holes of a sieve, and gaps in the leaves of trees produced the same effect. In fact, as early as the thirteenth century, mathematicians and astronomers used the phenomenon to safely observe solar eclipses.

For centuries this remained little more than an interesting novelty, but the power of the camera obscura was harnessed during the Renaissance like so much other ancient knowledge. Using a mirror to direct the image onto a piece of paper, artists could trace what they saw and more accurately capture proportion and perspective, leading to an increased understanding of the mechanisms of both. The introduction of lenses in the sixteenth century increased clarity of the image projected, but the level of detail captured remained entirely in the skill of the hand crafting the image. This issue was not resolved for several centuries.

Frenchman Nicéphore Niépce had developed an interest in lithographic printing, but he relied on his talented son to draw for him. When the younger Niépce was drafted into the French army in 1814, the elder Niépce was forced to seek other means to create his images. In 1816, he began to experiment with the recently discovered photoreactive properties of silver halide salts on paper and daylight contact exposures, just as Englishman Thomas Wedgwood had done some ten or twenty years earlier. Sadly, the images were only temporary; as soon as one exposed them to daylight, they quickly faded. For six years Niépce struggled with ways to make the images permanent, but the formulas with which he had so much previous success in their photoreactivity simply could not be permanently fixed.

In 1822, Niépce discovered the photoreactive properties of bitumen of Jordan, a naturally occurring tar-like hydrocarbon found in the Dead Sea. In 1826, he spread the mixture on a lithographic stone and for the first time used a camera obscura to focus sunlight onto it in a process he called *héliographie*. The result was the first permanent photographic lithograph, which Niépce unwittingly destroyed with further experimentation.

He repeated his experiments in 1827—or 1828, the exact date remains uncertain—this time spreading a bitumen-lavender oil solution on a sheet of pewter. Niépce pointed his camera out the window of his home in Le Gras for eight hours or more (some estimates claim Niépce exposed the plate for

Figure 1-9. An original daguerreotype in its pressed papier-mâché case. The silver photographic plate was coated with a mixture of photoreactive chemicals that resulted in a positive image on the silver. Once exposed over a dish of heated mercury, the vapors darkened the unexposed silver; the dark areas of the image are actually tarnished silver, and not part of the exposed image.

Figure 1-10. Another original daguerreotype in a case of pressed papier-mâché. Note that his cheeks have been tinted to give him a rosy complexion. Many early photographers were skilled portrait artists who entered as photographers into a world of black and white; they applied their painting abilities to add color when a sitter requested it.

as much as two full days). The process created a faint yet permanent positive image on the plate, but when he exposed the pewter to heated iodide crystals, the vapor darkened the unexposed pewter and increased the contrast until the faint image was much easier to see. Niépce's *View from the Window at Le Gras* became the world's first photograph.

In 1829, Niépce met an artist in Paris by the name of Louis-Jacques-Mandé Daguerre, who had been experimenting with capturing images with a camera obscura himself. The two formed a partnership, in which Daguerre's enthusiasm eclipsed Niépce's waning energy. When Niépce died in 1833, Daguerre was left with a promising, though not yet practical, starting point.

Daguerre knew Niépce's heliography had merit; the natural niello contrasted well with the bright, positive image areas on silver-plated copper sheets. The primary issue they had faced was not the quality of the images, but the exposure time; Niépce's heliography took six to eight hours, which was fine for most landscapes, but Daguerre wanted to make portraits. By 1837, he had perfected his process and began to show it around.

Thankfully, he had made a name for himself by showing his prototype images to his academic colleagues, because on March 8, 1839, his studio and nearly all of his photographs burned to the ground. With only a few remaining images to display, Daguerre described the process on August 19, 1839, step by step, to the Académie des Sciences and the Académie des Beaux-Arts, as well as throngs of spectators who had crowded into the galleries. Retaining his patents, Daguerre sold the rights for the process to the French government for a lifetime stipend, and the daguerreotype process became available to the world.

Daguerre was not the only one creating photographic history; an Englishman named Henry Talbot had been perfecting his own process. Like Niépce, he was experimenting with photoreactive chemicals and, in 1835, had created negatives from silver chloride–coated paper, from which he could create multiple positive contact prints. His problem had also been excessively long exposure times, but he was doubly troubled by a lack of resolution; Daguerre's images were much sharper and clearer than his.

In January 1839, Talbot announced the perfected process he called "photogenic drawing" to the Royal Society of London, which met with a lukewarm reception at best. Daguerre had already created a buzz about photography in France, and Talbot's images were shallow representations by comparison. By 1840, Talbot had reduced exposure times to mere seconds, rather than the minutes required of Daguerre's process (at that time), a development that he thought would draw interest away from Dageurre's procedure to his.

Patenting his process in 1841 under the name *calotype* (which he later humbly renamed *talbotype*), Talbot's improved procedure not only reduced exposure times even further but greatly increased resolution and image quality over his previous attempts. Unfortunately, the images still paled compared to those of Daguerre, whose longer exposure times resulted in a much-greater

Figure 1-11. This demure daguerreotype from the 1840s (full size) is not only interesting for its case and the image of a very pretty young woman, but because the image is set into the left side of the case. The majority of period photos, both daguerreotypes and glass plate photos, are placed on the right. It is possible that the owner of this image was left-handed.

Figures 1-12 and 1-13. Daguerre discovered that the smaller the plate, the shorter the exposure time, so daguerreotypes are rarely much larger than about 3 inches tall, especially for portraits. This dapper gentleman from the 1840s has been enlarged to roughly 125% of its original size; the gutta-percha case (*to the right*) is shown at full size.

depth of field and captured so much more detail than Talbot's calotypes. Additionally, Talbot's images still tended to noticeably fade over time.

The popularity of the daguerreotype during the 1840s was overwhelming. On the website of the Metropolitan Museum of Art in New York, Malcolm Daniel presents a clear understanding of precisely how popular:

> Ultimately portraiture came to account for the vast majority of daguerreotypes, fulfilling a deep-seated desire to capture and preserve the face of a beloved husband or wife, a soldier son at war, an infant on her deathbed, or even a favorite family dog. To judge by the economic record—more than five-and-a-half tons of silver were used by Parisian platemakers in one year—millions of daguerreotypes were produced, and most of them were portraits.

The art world took special notice of the new craft, now commonly referred to as *photography* (first coined by Brazilian artist Hércules Florence in 1834). Some condemned photography for the impact it would have on their lives as artists and on the art of portraiture itself, but others abandoned their paints to become a new category of craftsman (the daguerreotypist), and began to establish studios in major cities of the world. Because each image was unique, a certain degree of artistic ability for composition was required, as well as a scientific understanding of exposure times and chemistry, to create the gems of portraiture that so many daguerreotypes became.

Figures 1-14 and 1-15. Glass collodion or wet-plate photography processed an image the same way a daguerreotype did, by rendering the positive areas on a plate, not the negative. The collodion process relied on a dark substrate visible from behind the glass to create a positive image. The figure on the left shows how the plate appears with a dark backing (usually black velvet, paper, or lacquer); the one on the right shows how the plate appears without it, with nothing to create the contrast for a recognizable image. Both are shown at their original size.

Unfortunately, the very properties that made the daguerreotype unique would also ultimately lead to its demise; once the image was made, there was no way to replicate it. Copies of an image could not be made, whereas with Talbot's calotype one could. Still, Talbot's method lacked the detail of Daguerre's until London sculptor Frederick Scott Archer experimented with a whole new substrate that would completely replace the daguerreotype by 1860.

Archer, a member of the Calotype Photographic Club, wondered whether he would be able to reduce exposure times even further while increasing detail. Between 1850 and 1851, Archer tested a combination of potassium iodide and collodion—better known as nitrocellulose or "gun cotton"—on a sheet of glass, which was then soaked in a bath of silver nitrate. This "wet plate" collodion process allowed Archer to capture high-resolution negative images after an exposure of only a few seconds with as much detail as Daguerre's process. By 1853, Archer found that he could reverse the image by bleaching the plate in silver salts, creating a positive image on glass. Once placed over a dark color—either in a velvet-lined case or with a dark varnish backing—the image could be viewed normally.

This process had a number of immediate advantages. The first was that the thickness of the glass added a sense of depth to the image, in addition to the depth of field of the photo. The second was the exposure time; patrons would be required only to sit for two to three seconds to have their picture taken. (Most people today believe that the reason no one smiled in early photographs was because of long exposure times. While this may have been true for the earliest daguerreotypes, the primary reason why few smiled a broad, toothy grin was because of the social convention at that time. The belief was that showing one's teeth apart from common conversation made one appear as an uncultured goof, and sitters considered these formal portraits.)

Another advantage of the collodion process was the processing time; collodion images required very simple chemistry and could be developed, fixed, and presented to a customer in just a few minutes. One could have an image struck and leave with the completed photo in a gutta-percha or pressed papier-mâché case within half an hour.

Figures 1-16 and 1-17. Unlike daguerreotypes, glass plate photos are more prone to the extremes of heat and humidity. In the photo above, the image's emulsion is separating from the back of the glass, while the image of the figure below is shattering at the edges. (Each case is roughly 2 1/2" x 3")

Figures 1-18 and 1-19. This glass plate photograph was probably taken in the late 1850s or early 1860s. The patriotic pressed-paper case featuring George Washington, a displayed eagle, and two American flags could well have been purchased after the photo was taken, perhaps as a gift for a departing soldier.

If the customer wanted multiple copies of an image, the plate could remain unbleached and numerous positive paper images could be made from the glass negative. In 1854, Parisian photographer André Adolphe Eugène Disdéri devised a method to take several different poses on the same glass plate, print all eight poses onto a single sheet of photographic paper, cut them apart, and glue them onto preprinted cards. These photographic calling or visiting cards—known by their French name, *carte de visite*, commonly shortened to CDV by collectors today—were often about the size of a modern business card, though the term "CDV" is also used in Europe today to describe the larger gallery cards of the later nineteenth century.

Because so many images could be made and sold at very reasonable prices, cartes de visite of famous personages, locations, and works of art were printed and collected as souvenirs, either of foreign travels or as icons of admiration. CDVs of royalty—especially of Queen Victoria of England or Empress Eugénie of France, members of the royal families, or even members of their courts—were printed and sold across the world.

Figures 1-20 and 1-21. These original Disdéri cartes de visite, or CDVs as they're commonly known by collectors, were taken in one of his two Paris studios in the 1860s. Disdéri opened a London studio in 1865 and took a number of very popular pictures of Queen Victoria. Disdéri is also known for his photos of the 1870–71 siege of Paris.

Perhaps the most promising advantage of the collodion process was that, unlike Daguerre and Talbot, Archer did not patent his process, and he openly made the details free to any photographer. As a result, glass positive photos became immensely popular during the 1850s and lasted well into the 1880s. Commonly misnamed *ambrotypes*—a similar procedure that used a different fixative process patented by American James Ambrose Cutting in 1854—positive collodion images were created and sold by the millions.

The exact same process was used for *ferrotypes* (commonly known as tintypes in the United States). Instead of glass, a thin sheet of metal primed with black lacquer was similarly coated with the photoreactive mixture and developed the same way. Because the picture was on an already dark background, there was no need for a case, and many tintypes—so named because of the cheap, flimsy result when compared to pricey daguerreotypes and glass collodions—could be mounted on simple printed or embossed paper cards. First patented in 1857 by Hamilton Smith in the United States, tintypes continued to be

Figure 1-22. This large CDV of a social gathering in the late 1850s was made from a half-plate photograph (4¹/₄" x 5¹/₂"), trimmed and glued to a 5¹/₂" x 6¹/₂" decorative card. It's an unusual photo, not only because it is so large, but because it has so many people displayed at one sitting, which was not common at that time.

a popular, inexpensive photographic method for almost one hundred years, with street photographers in England making tintypes while one waited as late as the 1950s.

By 1860, photography had become so popular that the first commercially available products, such as precoated photographic paper, entered the market, but the medium remained ungainly. Because lenses allowed for little if any adjustment, the focal length required for an image to be crisply focused on the plate remained the primary determining factor for the size of a camera. As a result, cameras remained large, cumbersome boxes that required a tripod for steadiness. A person simply could not hold the large apparatus still enough long enough to get crisp images. Also, because plates had to be coated, used, and developed on-site, portable darkrooms, complete with noxious chemicals, had to be set up close to where one photographed.

Figures 1-23 and 1-24. Judging by the fullness of the sleeves on this young man's paletot coat, this German CDV from Rothenburg was probably taken in the mid-1860s. (Reverse has been reduced.)

Figure 1-25. This modern CDV of the author and his wife was taken by collodion artist Fritz Kirsch at the 1998 commemoration of the federal occupation of the Castillo de San Marcos National Monument in St. Augustine, Florida. Although horizontal formats were rare for original portraits, they were not unheard of. *Courtesy of Fritz Kirsch*

Figure 1-26. Probably the most popular early photographic format, the ferrotype is more commonly known as the tintype because of its cheap feel. Using photographic emulsion on black enamel-coated steel plates, tintypes required much-shorter exposure times. Unfortunately, they still required a willing (and still) subject to get a clear picture; the child in this photo was kicking his feet when this image was made.

Figure 1-27. This tintype of a rosy-cheeked woman was probably taken in 1863, judging by the cut of her striped bodice and full sleeves. Tintypes were popular mementos for departing soldiers on both sides of the war.

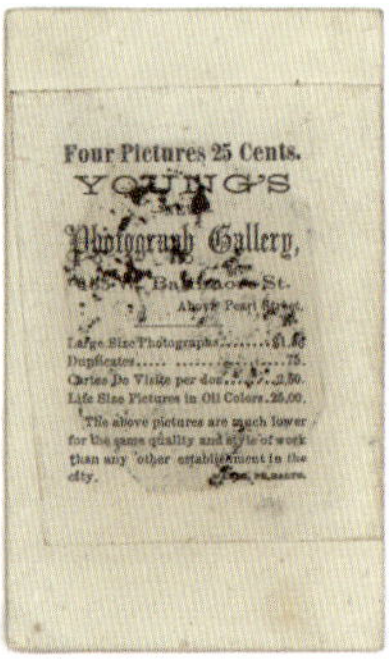


Figures 1-28 through 1-31. Tintypes were originally sold in commercially available printed or embossed paper frames. Because they were made of metal, the images themselves were far more durable than the frames, so between insects, weather, and time, the frames do not always survive. (approximately 2⁵/₈" x 4" each)

Figure 1-32. A resourceful photographer duplicated this photo from an album by taking a picture of it; the only way one could duplicate a print without the original negative plate.

Figure 1-33. Because tintypes were so cheap (note the prices advertised on the two frames in figures 1-30 and 1-31), there are a number of humorous originals available to collectors. This cigar-gnawing man in a derby props his chin on a painted placard, giving him the appearance of riding a sow like a steed. His fingers are visible on the left edge of the photo.

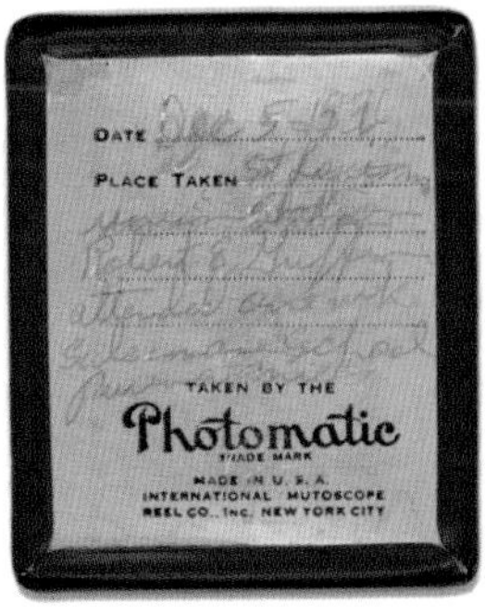


Figures 1-34 and 1-35. The tintype remained popular until the 1950s. This December 5, 1936, steel-framed tintype of the author's wife's grandfather, taken in a photo booth at St. Louis Union Station, is inscribed, “attended one wk salesman school purina [*sic*] mills.” (Back has been reduced.)

Figure 1-36. When they were not stored or displayed in paper or pressboard frames, CDVs, albumen prints, and tintypes were stored in family albums, such as this red velvet album from 1882. (approximately $8^{3}/_{4}$" x $10^{1}/_{2}$")

In 1871, Dr. Richard Leach Maddox of England proposed and experimented with a new process. This "dry-plate process" allowed for the preparation of plates far in advance of their use. Photographers soon discovered that by curing the gelatin emulsion with heat, the sensitivity of the plates increased dramatically, so much so that shorter exposure times no longer required tripods for stability; one could hold a camera and still get a clear photo.

By itself, Dr. Maddox's development was not particularly remarkable, but when combined with the discovery in 1887 of clear celluloid, the future was primed for a great leap forward. A gentleman by the name of George Eastman was in the perfect place at the perfect time to take advantage of it.

Figure 1-37. Because they could be printed en masse, CDVs made for great souvenirs. This 1888 view of Hohensalzburg Castle overlooking Salzburg, Austria, was taken from the Capuchin Monastery across the Salzach River. It remains a popular tourist attraction to this day.

Figures 1-38 and 1-39. One never knows what one will find at a yard sale; this $20 wooden box contained an original 1882-dated camera, complete with frame for photographic plates. The frame would be loaded with either a single glass or two tin plates (one on either side) and placed in the back of the camera. When the sliding wooden cover was opened, the plate was exposed by removing the lens cap for the requisite number of seconds, depending on emulsion and intensity of daylight. The camera is in such good condition that the coated canvas bellows is still light safe.

## From the Studio to the Snapshot

Eastman was a junior bookkeeper at Rochester Savings Bank in New York. In 1878, he made plans to travel to Santo Domingo to investigate a client's land speculation, but he needed some fashion of documenting his findings. On paper the deal looked promising, but he needed better proof to present to the bank, so he researched photography as his primary method to accomplish this. Eastman became so enamored with the burgeoning hobby that he started his own side business and opened Eastman Dry Plate Company in April 1880.

In 1881, Eastman read of a patent by French photographer Etienne-Jules Marey for a repeating camera, one that would permit multiple images on a single plate. This prompted Eastman to wonder if instead of taking multiple images on a single plate, could one create a way to take multiple images on multiple plates? He promptly tendered his resignation at Rochester Savings Bank.

Eastman shifted his research from glass plates to Talbot's paper plates, but using modern chemicals. Since paper was far more flexible than glass, he and fellow Eastman Company employee William Walker developed and patented the Eastman-Walker Roll Holder in 1885. This allowed the Eastman Company to produce a camera in 1888 that was preloaded with 20 feet of paper plates, enough for one hundred small, 2½" diameter images. Eastman had created a simple point-and-shoot camera; one only had to look through a viewport to frame a picture and click on the shutter button.

The new camera sold for only $25; a person could snap a hundred shots and then send the camera to the Eastman Company in Rochester, New York. The camera was then reloaded and returned to the customer while the roll was developed. His slogan, "You press the button, we do the rest," captured

Figure 1-40. Because people rarely had their image struck while wearing unfashionably older clothes, many photographs can be dated by the clothing the sitter is wearing. This woman from Dortmund, Germany, wears a dress that was popular between 1891 and 1893, so we can be reasonably assured this photo was taken within that time span. (2⁵/₈" x 4¹/₄")

Figure 1-41. Although Disdéri's CDVs were about the size of a modern business card, Europeans also continue to refer to larger photographic cards as CDVs. In North America, these larger photos, some as large as 5¹/₂" x 8¹/₂", are often referred to as cabinet or gallery cards. This card from Tondern, Germany (now Tønder, Denmark), dates from between 1901 and 1903. (2³/₄" x 4³/₈")

Figure 1-42. Conveniently dated on the back in 1905 by Carola Streit, this Berlin CDV was probably printed from a glass plate negative. Portrait studios continued to use larger cameras with tripods and the older, dry-plate processes instead of newer, smaller cameras. As complicated as the process was, studios preferred the sharper images they got from their older, stalwart cameras. (2⁵/₈" x 4¹/₄")

Figure 1-43. By 1905, when this picture was taken, Eastman's Kodak cameras were turning nearly everyone in the United States into a photographer. ($4^1/_2$" x $6^1/_8$")

the imagination of would-be photographers everywhere. No longer was one required to go to a photography studio; now *anyone* could be a photographer. George Eastman named the camera the Kodak—a short, easily memorized name that could not be mistaken for any other product on the market at the time—and he later admitted because he just liked the letter "K."

In 1889, Eastman created an even-better plate for his new camera, one that relied on a clear but flexible cellulose base instead of paper. Eastman had given Americans, and later the world, a new passion. Fascination with photography had given rise to clubs and associations, magazines, and other venues for devotees to vent their enthusiasm. In 1900, Eastman introduced the Kodak Brownie camera to the world for just $1, complete with a six-exposure roll of film available for only 15¢ per roll.

Around that same time, the German *Reisekamera* (travel camera) became increasingly popular in Europe. Looking more like a throwback camera of the 1880s than Eastman's latest models, the *Reisekamera* had a collapsible bellows that not only reduced the size of the camera for transportation but also permitted adjustment of the focal length. This allowed for much-larger, more-detailed images to be taken with smaller, easily portable cameras.

In 1907, a method for enlarging images in the darkroom was developed using what is called a photostatic enlarger. The size of the print was no longer dependent on the size of the negative and, as a result, was independent of the size of the camera. The clarity of the image was unfortunately still dependent on the quality of the lens.

Former Carl Zeiss optician and photography aficionado Oskar Barnack, manager of the research and development department for the German microscope company Ernst Leitz Optische Werke (Optical Works), embraced this new challenge for photography. Determined to create "small negatives,

Figure 1-44. As stated earlier, when people chose to sit for a photograph, they did so in their finer clothing. This older couple posed just after the turn of the nineteenth century (ca. 1902–1904), wearing clothing they might wear for a formal night out or a grand evening at the theater. What is especially interesting is how the studio trimmed the train of the woman's dress beyond the edge of the print yet still kept the white border intact. (4⅝" x 5⅜" photo on a 10" x 11⅞" background)

Figure 1-45. This is an interesting photo that is probably contemporaneous with the figure above, though one would not know by dating it from her clothing—an eighteenth-century-style Robe Anglaise—which may well have been original. The woman in the picture was either on her way to or had just returned from a costume party. (5⅝" x 6⅝")

Figures 1-46 and 1-47. As George Eastman's cameras caught on, new-found photography aficionados snapped pictures of everything they found of interest. Unfortunately, the images are not what others might find particularly fascinating, from the dirt road one lived on to the family dog. Still, the albums that Americans, and later Europeans, assembled would capture an era like none before, documenting the historic as well as the mundane and painting an image of the world unique to its time. (Each picture is approximately $2^{1}/_{4}$" square)

large prints," Barnack used much-higher-quality lenses to capture more detail on horizontally-wound 35 mm motion picture film. He developed what he called the Leica (short for Leitz camera) in 1913, but plans to commercially produce the pocket-sized camera were interrupted by the Great War. Following the war, Ernst Leitz II put Barnack's camera into production and, in 1924, released the now famous Leica I camera.

Other camera companies swiftly followed Leitz's example—even Kodak—and interest in amateur photography and personal snapshots increased exponentially. Small, handheld cameras with 35 mm film cartridges that could be loaded in daylight replaced box cameras (though not completely; Kodak's Brownie remained in production until the 1960s). Leitz also established a new innovation for photography in 1930, by introducing a

Figure 1-48. This oddly proportioned CDV ($2^{3}/_{4}$" x $5^{1}/_{4}$") of a German soldier of the 21st Regiment (Infantry?) was taken in 1916. As with photos from a half century earlier, small props were available in the studio for the sitter to lean on, stand beside, or otherwise make the area look less like a studio (note the painted canvas backdrop). Interestingly, the *soldat* is resting his hand on a photo album.

Figure 1-49. Social gatherings always provided a good excuse to bring out the camera. These ladies pose en masse circa 1913. (3⁵/₈" x 5⁵/₈")

Leica camera with interchangeable lenses. Different lenses allowed for varied focal lengths and apertures for different effects, all without requiring a different camera altogether.

There was still a small problem with the Leica and cameras like it: they relied on a viewfinder to frame the picture. Since the viewfinder was rarely in line with the lens through which the image was captured, the parallax angle often created photos in which the primary object of the picture was not centered. Frequently, an amateur photographer waited a week or more only to find out that the picture had "cut off" the subject at one or more edges of the photo.

Figure 1-50. This ad for Ernemann Feld-Kameras (field cameras) clipped from a 1916 magazine promises "the best successes on all theaters of the war," as well as a free price list with all transactions.

Figure 1-51. Ernst Leitz's Leica camera is quite possibly one of the best-known cameras of the 1920s. The Leitz company, renowned for its microscopes and optics, developed complex multiple lenses that allowed the Leica to take very sharp pictures on a small negative, giving birth to the 35 mm format for film.

Figure 1-52. The Zeiss-Ikon Ikonta camera, released in 1929, is advertised here as "a genuine joy to use" and even had a flip-down stand on the cover (visible above the word "Dresden") to steady the camera on a tabletop. At 35 reichsmarks, it was roughly the same price as Kodak cameras, but for Depression-era Germany it was not cheap. For the time, though, the Ikonta was relatively affordable and durable; there are a number of fully functional Ikonta cameras available on today's market. (5" x 6¾")

Figure 1-53. This 1932 ad from *Berliner Illustrierte Magazin* (*Berlin Illustrated Magazine*) introduced the Leica Model II, a camera that had a built-in range finder (*Entfernungsmesser*) for even sharper images than Barnack and Leitz's original design. (4½" x 6")

Figure 1-54. Leitz licensed manufacture of his cameras to other parts of the world, most notably the Soviet Union. Feliks Dzerzhinski, founder of the Soviet secret police, opened his own factory to make Russian Leicas but made enough changes and improvements to the design to call it his own camera, the FED (Dzerzhinski's initials). Based on the Leica Model II, the FED was also known as the NKVD camera (the initials of Dzerzhinski's secret police); this FED camera's serial number dates it to 1937.

The Industrie- und Handelsgesellschaft (Industry and Trade Society camera company, shortened to Ihagee, the German pronunciation for IHG) was one of the first of the new camera companies to solve this difficulty when it released a single lens reflex (SLR) camera—the Exakta—in 1933. By using an angled mirror in place of the shutter at the focal plane in front of the film, a photographer could view and frame the composition of an image through the lens, rather than around it, and see it just as it would be exposed on the film. By releasing the shutter mechanism, the mirror flipped up and out of the way, exposing the film, and then returned to its location for the next shot.

Other camera companies attempted to solve the parallax problem by using less complicated methods, such as the Rolleicord and Rolleiflex cameras made by Franke & Heidecke. This twin-lens reflex (TLR) camera relied on two lenses, one above the other; the photographer looked down to a mirror that reflected out the first lens, which acted as a viewfinder, while the second lens directly below it exposed the film. This arrangement solved some of the problems with parallax, but when interchangeable lenses became available for SLR and viewfinder cameras, most TLR cameras could not be adapted to accept the new lenses and so decreased in popularity.

## The Shutter Bug Bites the Reich

These smaller, handheld cameras were immensely popular throughout Germany, both as a hobby and as a source of national pride, as Leitz and other German companies established themselves as technological leaders of the industry.

Figure 1-55. This 1936 ad for the Zeiss-Ikon Super Ikonta 6x6 large-format camera boasted a larger negative for sharper images, while still remaining a handheld camera that was easy to use. The copy above suggests that the Super Ikonta 6x6 was the perfect camera for taking sharp, close-up pictures of winter plants and enjoying them from the warmth of one's house. (6 1/8" x 8 1/8")

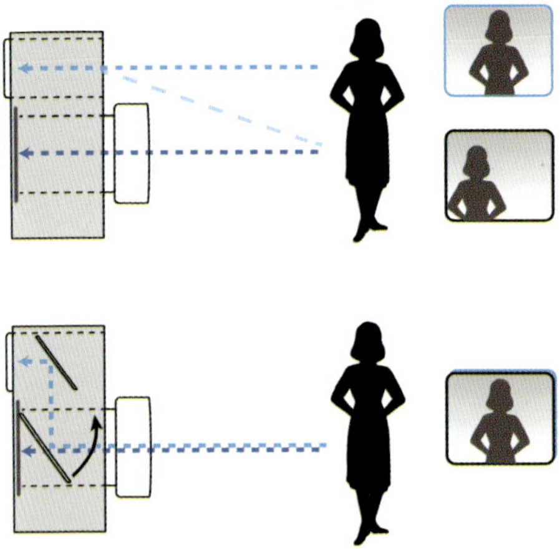

Figures 1-56 and 1-57. A problem with handheld cameras of the time was that the viewfinder was rarely in line with the lens, so the parallax angle created by the difference in what the lens saw and what the photographer saw (*above*) often made framing the subject difficult. The single-lens-reflex (SLR) camera used a mirror as part of the shutter mechanism; the photographer viewed the shot through the lens and the mirror-shutter flipped out of the way to expose the film. The Ihagee Exakta camera pictured in this 1940 ad was the first true SLR camera; it was released in 1933. (3¼" x 4⅛")

Figure 1-58. Not to be outdone by the photographic technology boom in Germany, Kodak introduced its Retina camera with a built-in light meter and range finder for the perfect exposure and focus for "only" 155 reichsmarks. (4¾" x 8")

Figure 1-59. While Ihagee established the market for the single-lens reflex camera, Franke & Heidecke developed the twin-lens reflex Rolleicord and Rolleiflex cameras. The photographer looked straight down into the viewfinder, into a mirror, and out of the upper lens, while the lower lens was reserved for exposing the film. The immediate advantage was that it was a much less complicated system than the SLR camera; although it allowed for centered photos left and right, it only reduced the parallax and did not eliminate it. This ad ran in *Berliner Illustrierte Magazin* in 1939. (approximately 5⁵/₈" x 11")

But it was the Nationalsozialistische deutsche Arbeiterpartei (the NSDAP or Nazi Party) that took a particular interest in photography. Identifying the approaching trend and positioning themselves to take advantage of it, the Nazis created their own film department in 1930. Since Dr. Josef Goebbels's appointment as national director of propaganda for the party, the Nazis had presented a carefully crafted image to the people. They soon came to rely on amateur photos its members had donated, as well as those posed and taken by professionals to support that image; candid, spontaneous shots of the party's supporters were very convincing, and this expanded use of the media resulted in an expanded message.

The party encouraged this newfound love of photography, both as an economic incentive—more photographers bought more cameras—and as a cultural record of Germany itself. State-sponsored photographic exhibitions and competitions allowed the party to select winners thematically for ideological value, encouraging positive depictions of German culture and discouraging critical portrayals of the Reich. The result was a de facto propaganda campaign unwittingly waged upon the people of Germany by the people themselves.

Germans took to documenting their lives through pictures at a rapid pace, noting any occasion worthy of merit: birthdays, religious confirmations, weddings, and even picnics, club gatherings, and family dinners. During the

Figure 1-60. Technological advancements in 1930s Germany made amateur photography extremely popular throughout Europe, but especially within the Reich. Citizens documented everything and kept meticulous albums, from the brown *Sturmabteilung* (Storm Trooper or SA) album (*on the left*) to the red Bund deutscher Mädel (Organization of German Maidens or BDM, the female equivalent to the Hitler Youth), *on the right*.

Figure 1-61. The pages of the Bund deutsche Mädel (BDM) album (*above*) document this girl's days at camp, a photojournalistic record that was kept instead of a diary or journal. The Nazi Party encouraged photographic journals, which became de facto propaganda for their cause.

Figure 1-62. This loose page from a Heer Helferin's journal—a female Army auxiliary "helper"—documents her service in France in 1941. An assignment in occupied France was almost regarded more as a working vacation than a duty station, as one can see by the relaxed and recreational atmosphere.

1930s, film and photography clubs appeared everywhere, as did photography journals, magazines, and books. Germans owned five to six million cameras by 1936—roughly 10 percent of the population—and by 1939 that number had climbed to seven million. Photo albums and scrapbooks of all sizes were available at studios, bookstores, and department stores, and Germans bought and filled them.

## Photography and the War

This practice did not stop with the coming of the war. German families photographed one another, and the *soldat* wasted no time in doing the same with his new family: his fellow soldiers. Small albums specifically marketed to the Wehrmacht and other services, such as the Reichsarbeitsdienst (RAD, National Labor Service), labeled "*Erinnerung an meine Dienstzeit*" (Souvenir of My Time in the Service), were decorated with motifs of helmets, crossed rifles, or Nazi Party eagles. Soldiers purchased, carried, and filled them with snapshots of *Kameraden* with whom they ate, trained, and fought. *Soldaten* carried an estimated 100,000 cameras to the eastern front alone, often choosing to create photographic records of their service in lieu of written journals or diaries.

Cameras continued to be manufactured and sold throughout the war.

Figure 1-63. These ads from the September 1, 1942, issue of *Der Adler* (The Eagle)—a trade publication for the Luftwaffe—prominently features an ad for Adox Foto Company, the oldest photochemical company in the world at that time. Adox, Hauff, and Agfa were the primary producers of photochemicals when there was a shortage of many other goods in Germany. (approximately 6½" x 9⅜")

Germany did not change its industry over to a wartime footing until 1942, ceasing the production of consumer goods to concentrate on weapons and wartime necessities. Yet, advertisements for cameras, particularly Zeiss-Ikon, Leica, and Rolleicord/Rolleiflex, continued to be inserted in magazines until many went out of print at the end of the war. Germany could not produce the fighters it needed in 1945, but it had no shortage of cameras.

Most photos were taken early in the conflict, with a noted decline beginning in the middle of 1944, but pictures were taken and developed throughout the war (though some film was almost certainly developed afterward). One would expect that given the privations and shortages Germans experienced from 1943 to 1945, the photochemical industry would have also suffered, but this does not appear to be the case.

In Hans Neumann's 1953 book *Neuzeitlich Vergrössern* (Latter-Day Enlarging),

Figure 1-64. This small classified ad for photo developing and prints ran in the September 27, 1943, issue of *Spandauer Zeitung* (Spandau Newspaper), from the Berlin suburb. Though the hours were limited (2:00 p.m. to 5:00 p.m.), and even then only on Mondays and Saturdays, Fotograf Leske remained open despite shortages, bombing, and the war.

his formula for mixing a batch of developer in 1944 differed very little from prewar recommendations. In fact, the Metol solution is even stronger than what was recommended in the 1930s, implying no need to skimp for lack of supply or increased price. Given that so many goods in Germany were scarce at best, this comes as a bit of a shock. (In fact, Neumann's 1944 formula uses an even-stronger concentration of Metol than what is recommended today, though that is primarily due to modern health concerns.) This supports claims that, even given the lack of the most basic requirements within the Reich, such as food and clothing, photochemicals—of all things—were still widely available.

Photography in Germany during the 1940s primarily relied on silver halides for film emulsions, Metol and hydroquinone by Hauff Photochemische Fabrik (Photochemical Factory) and Agfa's Rodinal for film developers, acetic acid for stop bath solutions, and ammonium or sodium thiosulfate as a fixative. Most of these chemicals could be manufactured or synthesized from naturally occurring ingredients—some, such as acetic acid, from agricultural waste—so the impact on the production of strategic industrial chemicals was minimal. Most importantly, demand was high enough to maintain production, not just for amateur photographers and developing studios, but by the Nazi Party itself.

The party or, rather, the Propaganda Ministry relied very heavily on motion pictures to continue its message. The final issue of the *Deutsche Wochenschau*—the German weekly newsreel that was the equivalent of American *Movietone News*—was not released to theaters until March 1945, when roughly half the country was already in Allied hands. In late 1943 and into 1944, Goebbels authorized filming of the movie *Kolberg*, about the city's stand against Napoleon. The ministry spent eight million reichsmarks (more than half a billion dollars today) and diverted 187,000 extras—some 50,000 of whom were Wehrmacht troops—6,000 horses, and 10,000 specially made uniforms for the film.

Hauff, the company that manufactured Metol, was in Stuttgart, which suffered fifty-three air raids during the war (most of them in 1944), the worst of which caused a firestorm on September 12. However, this affected only the immediate production of Metol, hydroquinone, and glycin (all three of which were used for developing prints). These chemicals, when stored dry, have shelf lives of up to fifty years. If a professional or amateur darkroom already had an adequate stock set aside, even the Stuttgart firestorm of September 1944 would not have affected film developing for the remainder of the war. In fact, it appears as though the only developer affected was Agfa's Rodinal. At the beginning of the war, limited supplies of sodium sulphites endangered the production of Rodinal, but when Agfa substituted potash for soda in 1940, manufacture continued unabated.

Throughout the war, *soldaten* sent rolls of film home to be developed. Family members pasted some photos into albums but returned the remainder to the front, where they might be traded for tobacco, sweets, or other items to those without cameras, or just given to friends as gifts or souvenirs. It is important to note that the undeveloped rolls of photos taken at the front and sent home were rarely censored. The camera played an important role in *soldats*' lives and created an "unofficial" record of the Wehrmacht, one that was not at all flattering, then or now.

The sights of war, bombed buildings, damaged and destroyed vehicles, and dead livestock, enemy soldiers, and civilians were just a few of the common themes of destruction and death that *soldaten* shared with their families. Photos from the eastern front were especially brutal and even showed images of executions and pogroms in grim detail, above and beyond the over two million images recorded officially by *Kriegsberichter* (war reporters).

It comes as no surprise that lighthearted and comical photographs, such as those collected here, had become so popular.

Figures 1-65 and 1-66. Both of these ads ran in the September 1, 1943, issue of *Signal Magazine*, the German equivalent in size and content to *Life* in the United States. Camera ads continued to run in many magazines and newspapers until the very end of the war, not only as a public-awareness branding campaign, but also to advertise the availability of their products, regardless of the shortages of other goods. (5" x 6¼" each)

Figure 2-1. Only about 2 inches tall, this charming little plastic figurine from 1955 commemorates the centennial of the *cantinières'* service during the Crimean War. Between 1850 and 1870, *cantinières* served with distinction from the Crimea to the Franco-Prussian War until they were disbanded and eventually forgotten like so many other veterans of the nineteenth century.

# 2

# Women in Uniform as a Photographic Theme

With the exception of the women who served in limited frontline military service in antiquity and as noncombative and support roles throughout history, it was only at the close of the eighteenth century that women first entered uniformed service in the military. Beginning in 1793, and throughout the Napoleonic wars, women served as *cantinières* and *vivandières* (the terms were not exclusive and were often interchangeable) in the French army (La Grande Armée). *Cantinières* (canteen staff) and *vivandières* (licensed businesswomen, or wives/daughters of regimental victualers and nonmilitary supply contractors) often wore modified regimental uniforms that matched that of the regiments they served (whether these regiments issued them remains to be proven).

They frequently served to deliver water to the men on the march, as well as tend to the wounded with water or brandy during combat. They were not prostitutes or camp followers, although a number of them were wives of soldiers or officers. The *cantinière* service continued beyond the defeat of Napoleon, and women served with distinction during the Algerian Campaign of 1836.

Perhaps inspired by tales of uniformed women from the Napoleonic wars, Gaetano Donizetti wrote an opera about an orphaned little girl discovered on the battlefield and raised by a regiment of French grenadiers, *La fille du régiment* (*The Daughter of the Regiment*). First performed in Paris in 1840, the production received poor reviews, especially from its primary critic Hector Berlioz, who cared little for Donizetti personally. By 1844, the opera had grown in popularity somewhat but was wildly received almost immediately in the United States and England and played repeatedly throughout both countries until 1847.

In a case of life following art, in 1853 the New York 7th Regiment adopted the orphaned daughter of Maj. Joseph Divver, a popular officer who served with distinction during the Mexican-American war, only to meet an untimely demise on his return. Each member contributed a dollar a year toward her care and education, and when she, like Donizetti's heroine, "came of age, though mistress of a thousand hearts, she deserted to an enemy who offered her only one." *Scribner's Monthly* of 1880 subsequently reported, "now, the Daughter of the Regiment is mother to a small regiment of her own" (Holland 1880, p. 69).

English and French armies joined the Ottoman Empire in 1853, to fight Russia in the Crimean War (which lasted until 1856), and Donizetti's premise was once again news. To the French, who had sent at least two generations of women to the front lines by that point, there was nothing amiss, but to the British, who had permitted wives to join their husbands on campaign but had done little to accommodate them, the sight of women in uniform came as a shock.

*Cantinières* were as well kempt as French soldiers themselves, maintaining their uniforms with every bit as much pride as those of their regiments, and had specific duties to fulfill and regulations governing their behavior. Their uniforms were styled after their respective regiments, complete with trousers, in an era where such cross-dressing was illegal in many nations, even France. Compared to the disheveled British wives they cut dashing figures, especially when they rushed forward to tend to the wounded.

Both blue and gray armies followed suit during the American Civil War (1861-65), unofficially adopting the precedent established by their French counterparts. Both sides enlisted *cantinières* and *vivandières*, though the majority of the enlistees served in the Union Army of the Potomac in the eastern theater. Affectionately dubbed the "Daughter of the Regiment" by troops, the women were for all intents and purposes female mascots, but every bit as welcomed a sight on the march and to wounded soldiers as their French inspirations had been nearly a decade earlier. The Smithsonian Institution has an original *cantinière's* uniform as part of its Civil War collection.

The brutality of the conflict swiftly escalated; both sides soon realized that the modern battlefield presented far too hazardous a condition for women, and by the middle of 1862, both sides had dispensed with such niceties. Even though the women proved themselves to be as tough and brave as their male counterparts, Gen. Grant prohibited the practice entirely in September 1864. Women continued to serve on a strictly volunteer basis, but as civilians, and not as a part of a uniformed service.

Tales of women who had disguised themselves as men during the Civil War abounded on both sides, and over 300 documented cases exist of women who not only served in uniform as men but collected government pensions following the war. A few images are available of these women wearing the uniforms they wore under the guise of men; the ones that do exist are mostly postwar, but they are obviously women who are no longer attempting to disguise themselves.

It is doubtful whether these images encouraged the air of mystique that surrounded a woman in a man's uniform, but studio photographs and case photos of women wearing men's uniforms do begin to emerge at approximately the same time during the 1880s. The advent of widespread advertising and marketing toward the end of the nineteenth century also seemed to have taken advantage of the popularity of this trend.

Figure 2-2. The press was fascinated by French *cantinières* during the Crimean War and ran numerous pictorial articles about them. Illustrations often depicted demure damsels tending the wounded well out of harm's way, though according to firsthand accounts, they were as brave as any soldier—sometimes braver—dashing to tend the wounded under fire and hardly the pretty, petite maidens shown in the illustrations above. (approximately 11" x 16")

Figure 2-3. This large cartoon print addresses what one artist considered a great conundrum; namely, offering brandy or other "liquid fortifications" to teetotaling Turkish soldiers, who were Muslim. Prompting that the libation "would not hurt him," the French and British soldiers seem confused about their comrade's reticence. (approximately 9$^3/_4$" x 13$^3/_8$")

Figures 2-4. The *cantinière* became a popular marketing symbol in Europe and in the United States well into the twentieth century. This French trade card for chicory has turned the daunting heroine into a brand name, the Chicory of the French Cantinière. According to the slogan on the back, "although it is expensive, it is not as expensive as using more of the other brands," presumably for a comparable full flavor.

The "Daughter of the Regiment" became a very popular and successful marketing theme; whimsical illustrations of women in men's uniforms made their way not only into mainstream advertising, but also onto sheet music, political pamphlets, postcards, and other print venues. A woman in uniform, selling everything from soap to cigarettes, was never far from view on any given day.

This new image of a woman in men's clothing—particularly clothing that defined the epitome of masculinity, the military uniform—met with a great deal of societal consternation. Cross-dressing was still illegal in many European nations, and there were stiff penalties meted out to transgressors. Because the uniform represented a symbol of power in a patriarchal society, some considered the thought of a woman wearing a uniform comically absurd, while others believed it to be a very real threat. Most, at the very least, thought it a little erotic. So long as a woman wore a uniform only momentarily for the camera, or was the subject of a fanciful drawing, one could argue

Figures 2-5. This small promotional card for Duke's Cigarettes depicted fancy ball costumes–in this case the Daughter of the Regiment costume–complete with drumlike hat. By listing the different costumes on the back, the cards prompted smokers to purchase more to complete their set. (shown at 150% of original size)

Figure 2-6 (*left*). Though not always an advertising slogan, the Daughter of the Regiment remained a very popular artistic motif. This 1907 picture postcard of a young girl wearing a Civil War–era kepi and military-inspired medallion was a common commemorative to send during Decoration Day–precursor to Memorial Day–in which the graves of Civil War dead were decorated with flags and flowers. ($3^7/_8$" x $5^7/_8$")

Figure 2-7 (*right*). Another Daughter of the Regiment postcard (1911) sported embossed military motifs and silver metallic ink. This card was also printed as a commemorative for Decoration Day. ($3^7/_8$" x $5^7/_8$")

Figure 2-8. Starting in the 1880s, photographs of women wearing men's uniforms begin to emerge into the public eye. This woman wearing an Austro-Hungarian uniform complete with a medal bearing the likeness of Emperor Franz Josef was photographed for a *Korrespondenzkarte* (correspondence card). (3 5/8" x 5 1/2")

Figure 2-9. This woman, wearing a dress uniform and carrying a saber, was photographed in the Dutch city of Utrecht. (approximately 4" x 6")

that such offenses had been undertaken only for the sake of art and authorities tended to turn a blind eye.

During the late nineteenth and early twentieth centuries, female modernists donned elaborate costumes as symbols of freedom from the societal definition of femininity. While some considered men's clothes just another costume, others regarded a man's suit as the exemplification of freedom itself.

Women's-rights movements in the United States started in 1848, at the Seneca Falls Convention, and forty years later in Europe, at the International Council of Women in 1888. Dressing in men's clothes had become a bold political statement by the 1890s, one that was not lost on husbands and politicians. The idea that a woman would aspire to the same basic privileges enjoyed by men was foreign to them. In their minds, for a woman to wear a man's suit was a threat not just to male dominance, but to the fabric of society as a whole; the symbol of a desire to upset the whole "natural order" of civilization (an interesting accusation, since most civilizations began in Neolithic times as matriarchal).

Women's suffrage was a hotly debated topic across the Western world during the decades bracketing the turn of the nineteenth century, so the sight of women in men's clothing carried a great deal more political significance than what we would consider today. Captains of industry, bankers, and political leaders all wore business suits—the de facto uniform of their social strata as well as their economic position, which set them apart from the working class. For a woman to wear a business suit was tantamount to an assumption of that station, which was no more permissible than for a plumber or steelworker; it was an unacceptable appropriation of a social position, not merely a choice of clothing. It comes as no surprise then that symbolic imagery such as the "Daughter of the Regiment" as a marketing theme became so popular; women regarded the illustrations as a powerful symbol of what might be, while men were drawn to them because they were considered a bit kinky.

Figure 2-10. Women's rights, particularly voting rights, was a controversial topic at the end of the nineteenth and beginning of the twentieth century. This reproduction "Votes for Women" cockade by CreativeCockades.com was inspired by an original at the Museum of London. *Courtesy Heather Sheen*

Between 1900 and 1914, numerous images appeared of European women wearing men's uniforms, though these are often staged studio portraits and gallery photos as opposed to impromptu personal snapshots; amateur photography had yet to become universally popular, though it was well on its way. Although photographs of women in men's uniforms were prevalent across Europe, the majority of them appear to have been taken in Germany, the Austro-Hungarian Empire, and France. Most of the images portrayed dress and parade uniforms, though field uniforms (sometimes complete with pack and rifle) were not uncommon.

In the early years of World War I, photos of women in men's uniforms were lighthearted and farcical. The "Lonely *Poileau*" and "Fräulein Feldgrau" themes are more reminiscent of a home-front vision of military life, a world of barracks hijinks and pleasant camaraderie, rather than the merciless bloodbath that the

Figure 2-11. In this 1906 portrait, these women wear the uniforms of Infantry Regiment 68. It is not clear whether the uniforms belong to their husbands, sons, or brothers, but the amused looks on their faces lead one to wonder about the circumstances surrounding this photograph.

trenches had become in reality. Photo postcards were popular throughout the war, many calling upon patriotic themes, as well as the sexual undertones of women appealing to national causes.

During World War I, women once again served as uniformed members of the armed forces, though not in frontline service. Their uniforms were similar in cut to that of men but were frequently tailored to their figures—not to mention the use of skirts as opposed to trousers. Still, these were very obviously women's uniforms, not men's, and photos of uniformed women during the Great War are easily distinguishable from women wearing men's uniforms.

Figure 2-12. A hunting party takes a brief respite in this pre–World War I photo postcard. No one seems particularly pleased to be posing for the picture, especially not the woman in the foreground wearing the Deutches Heer uniform and cradling the hunting rifle, though the youngster in the back is scrunching his face in what could be one of the first photobombs. ($3^5/_8$" x $5^1/_2$")

Figure 2-13. This woman wearing a prewar/early-war uniform was taken in what appears to be the family sun room in her Weidensessel, a rattan wicker armchair. Definitely not a studio portrait, this rare early snapshot was taken long before amateur photography was widely popular in Germany. ($3^3/_4$" x $5^7/_8$")

Figure 2-14. These two ladies have chosen to represent Infantry Regiment 25 (note the embroidered epaulets). The woman on the right is wearing a uniform with capped sleeves usually reserved for a musician.

Figure 2-15. Gudrun Hildebrandt was a well-known German dancer at the turn of the nineteenth century whose journalist father worked for Kaiser Wilhelm II. Because she was so popular following her numerous appearances on postcards, she managed to transition very well into early German silent films. In this 1910 postcard, she wears a stylized hussar's uniform and raises her glass "To Good Comradeship!" (3⁵/₈" x 5⁵/₈")

Figure 2-16. "Fräulein Feldgrau" (Miss Field-Grey) was a popular motif on German postcards just prior to and during World War I. Mailed on September 16, 1915, this photo postcard was only one of a number of different women, all in uniform. The originals of photos for many postcards were hand tinted, then printed traditionally. (3¼" x 5¼")

Figure 2-17. Another Fräulein Feldgrau postcard, this one with most of her early war uniform visible, issues a confident slogan, "Dear Fatherland, you may rest easy." Something that many *soldaten* would have picked up on is the fact that the woman in the photo is not wearing a ring and could well be available, should they ever meet. Such was the fantasy of many a soldier. (3⅜" x 5⅝")

Figures 2-18 through 2-22. Donnerwetter Tadellos was another motif that was popular prior to the Great War. It is the title of a 1908 song and short film about the comically difficult life of a Berlin traffic policeman and is considered one of the first "talkies," though the sound was played from a record that was started at the same time as the movie; it was not a synchronized soundtrack. The title is an idiomatic expression best translated to "darn" flawless (literally "thunderstorms" flawless!). Some cards were hand tinted (though not exceptionally well) and printed in color, and some in black and white, but many of them featured a woman in military uniform, not a police officer. Figures 2-18 through 2-20 ($3\frac{1}{2}$" x $5\frac{3}{8}$") were printed in 1909; figures 2-21 and 2-22 (approximately $3\frac{1}{2}$" x $5\frac{1}{2}$") were printed in 1915 and 1916, respectively. Note the differences in uniforms.

Figures 2-23 and 2-24. Women were also depicted in uniform for themes of comradeship and patriotism. This postcard from 1916 asks, "Who could resist us?," while the 1917 card (*right*) seems intended to bolster the spirits and determination of *soldaten* at the front. The note at the bottom of the envelope reminds him who he is fighting for, that the lovely woman's "thoughts are with you," complete with Imperial Germany's colors. (approximately 3½" x 5½" each)

Figures 2-25 and 2-26. Not all photographs were taken in studios; snapshots of loved ones in uniform do exist from the Great War, though they are somewhat rare. Those who owned cameras were often eager to replicate the popular postcards. (2½" x 3¾" and 3⅝" x 5⅝", respectively)

Most Western countries recognized women's suffrage between 1918 and 1920 (though Great Britain withheld the right to vote on completely equal terms as men until 1928, and France did not permit women to vote at all until 1944). A woman in men's clothing lost a good deal of the symbolism it had held just a few years earlier, but not entirely. French athlete Violette Morris filed a lawsuit against the French Federation of Feminine Sports in the 1920s for withdrawing her license to wear trousers. Morris's life reads like a spin-off of Blake Edwards's *Victor Victoria* (1982), being an openly lesbian woman who adopted a very masculine lifestyle. Marlene Dietrich's lusty, tuxedo-clad Amy Jolly in *Morocco* (1930) and photographs of Katharine Hepburn wearing trousers created minor scandals in the US when they first appeared.

Figures 2-27 and 2-28. Company photographs were popular on both sides of the trenches during the Great War. This picture of the 7th Zug of the Leichte Minenwerfer Kompanie (7th Platoon of the Light Mortar Company) is a typical example. In figure 2-33 (*below*), the women of the "Battaillions [*sic*] Schneiderei" (battalion tailors' section) of Infantry Regiment 48 pose as a souvenir of their service between 1914 and 1917. By the time this picture was taken, soldiers had come to be known not only by their uniform, but also by their love of cigarettes. (both are 3½" x 5½")

Figure 2-29. During the Great War, English soldiers occasionally fancied a woman in battle dress. This English woman wears a 1902-style infantry uniform, one that was abandoned early in the conflict for one more practical. ($3\frac{3}{8}$" x $5\frac{3}{8}$")

Figure 2-30. This dainty Poileau seems more than happy to pose for her photographer. Happily puffing on her pipe, this mademoiselle wears a 1915-era French uniform. ($2\frac{5}{8}$" x $3\frac{7}{8}$")

Figure 2-31. Eager to capitalize on the United States' entry into the war, this 1917 postcard features a pipe-puffing woman in a US Army uniform, though the person who purchased it was French (note the inscription on the left). American soldiers and Marines were more interested in French souvenirs, not American. ($3\frac{5}{8}$" x $5\frac{1}{2}$")

Figure 2-32. Still, American soldiers were equally amused by the sight of women wearing men's uniforms, as this photo of two women (American? French?) in US uniforms attests. ($2\frac{5}{8}$" x $3\frac{5}{8}$")

These might have been considered mere publicity stunts, had it not been for the fact that these women were strong, determined celebrities whose masculine "take charge" attitudes were superseded only by their femininity. Hepburn's tomboyish behavior off-screen, as well as tales of Morris's and Dietrich's "exploits," heightened the erotic draw of a woman in men's clothing. The perception of a societal threat was still there, but considerably less than what it had been.

By the 1940s, the shock had worn off, especially as women reentered factories (women had worn trousers in some factories during the Great War, but only then under mid-calf-length skirts). Skirts continued to be de rigueur for female uniforms, but only for dress and office uniforms; women's work on flight lines, in factories, at antiaircraft emplacements, and at shipyards often required trousers or one-piece jumpsuits.

At the end of the Great War, most everyone had seen their fill of uniforms and wanted to be done with the thought of armed conflict ever again. The frequency of photographs both of men and women in uniform diminished during the 1920s but did not disappear entirely; the prevalent attitude was that the "War to End All Wars" had made the uniform passé. This was not the case in Germany.

Figure 2-33. Germans celebrated the Armistice as eagerly as the Allied nations, as this late 1918 postcard shows. Many would find their joy short lived once the terms of the Treaty of Versailles were announced and enforced. ($3\frac{5}{8}$" x $5\frac{1}{2}$")

Figure 2-34. This American woman wears a US Navy jumper. During the 1920s, when this picture was taken, few were interested in uniforms of any kind; the interest of taking pictures of women in men's uniforms dropped off. ($2^3/_4$" x $4^1/_2$")

Figures 2-35. Although the photo of this woman might lead one to think she wears a man's uniform, she is actually wearing her own. The Reichspost employed a number of women, both during the Great War and into the 1920s, and issued them uniforms similar to what the military wore, complete with leggings for inclement weather. ($3^3/_4$" x $5^1/_2$")

Because the Treaty of Versailles had so limited military service, membership in uniformed German civilian and paramilitary services grew immensely. Uniforms for these services went far beyond a common shirt or hat; they often included military-style jackets and trousers, belts, and various accoutrements. Uniforms were not only issued to the Reichsbahn (Rail Service), streetcar and subway services (*S-bahn* and *U-bahn*), and the postal service, but civilian lifesaving clubs, hunting organizations, and many others. Jobs were in extremely short supply, but Germans gathered to those services not only because they were hiring, but because of a sense of nationalistic duty that the uniform represented. As a result, one often finds images of women in nonmilitary uniforms in Germany from the 1920s and into the 1930s, as the trend continued. It is often difficult to determine whether these uniforms were those of their husbands and boyfriends or their own, since the cut of these uniforms was not particularly distinct between genders.

Nazi Germany was far more egalitarian than either the Weimar or imperial governments, much like communist Russia, but unlike her Russian counterpart, the German woman was still expected to maintain a traditionally demure decorum. Women of the Reich were welcomed into the Flugmeldedienst (Air Tracking Service) in 1930, into the Reichsluftschutzbund (National Air Defense Organization) in 1934, and as air raid wardens as early as 1935 yet were still pressured by the party to fulfill their roles as mothers and keepers of the hearth. For a woman to break completely with feminine tradition and responsibility, so far as the party defined them, was *streng verboten* (quite forbidden).

Immediately prior to the onset of World War II, when many could read the handwriting on the wall, the frequency of photos of women in uniform

Figures 2-36 through 2-38. During the 1930s and '40s, a number of German women wore uniforms of their own, which can make identifying those who wore their husbands' uniforms difficult. These *Schaffnerinnen* (female conductors for the Reichsbahn, the state railway system), *U-bahn* (subways), and Strassenbahn (street railways or trolleys) all wear uniforms as part of their regular positions, specifically collecting fares and punching tickets (note the ticket punchers at the end of their chains). The armband on the woman on the right in figure 2-38 indicates she is a member of the RAB Kriegshilfsdienst, the Reichsautobahn (state highway) War Assistance Service.

In the late 1930s and early in World War II, the fad of taking photos of women in men's uniforms regained popularity; a number of pictures exist of women wearing French men's uniforms. After June 1940, few uniforms apart from German ones were seen; the majority of French soldiers were taken prisoner and effectively held hostage as POWs in Germany.

Figure 2-39. This image of a young soldier and woman "reporting" for duty in 1937 is indicative of the enthusiasm with which Frenchmen responded, despite the government's reluctance. (approximately 2³/₈" x 4")

Figure 2-40. In this photograph from 1940, a French woman is resplendent in her husband's uniform, complete with tasseled garrison cap, crop, and cigarette.

Figure 2-41. Per the slogan of this 1940 postcard, the "pretty artillerist" has "reached my heart." (3¹/₂" x 5¹/₂")

increased, primarily in Germany and France. Nationalistic pride swelled in much the same way as it had prior to the Great War, and all were eager to display their enthusiasm. With the opening of hostilities, everyone came to the harsh realization that this war would be quite different from the last.

Once Germany occupied France, images of French women wearing men's uniforms understandably disappear until after Liberation in 1944–45. Comparatively few images exist of British Commonwealth women, and once the United States entered the war, this trend migrated across the pond only in limited instances.

A man's uniform was as much a symbol of power and authority as it always had been, so it continued to be usurped in the name of levity, not as a threat perceived or otherwise. By 1944, when the Allied air offensive in Germany had become so intense that German women not only were permitted to serve on flak crews but were even drafted for them, the uniforms they wore were their own. Now, as major contributors to the defense of the Reich, women's uniforms had become a symbol of their acceptance of collective responsibility.

There are few photographs of women wearing men's uniforms from the Soviet Union, but that does not mean they did not exist. One explanation for the scarcity of such photos is that women's uniforms and men's were all but identical in the Red Army, so it would be difficult to distinguish whether a woman was wearing her husband's uniform or her own. The other is that not as many personal snapshots seem to have been taken in the Soviet Union during that time; this is not because Russians were not as fond of photography, just that wartime limitations and communist rule made development of film a far lower priority than during peacetime. Following the end of the war, snapshots of personal celebrations and Black Sea vacations became quite common.

Figure 2-42. This woman wears a US Navy "cracker jack" uniform and dances a hornpipe in this photo from 1939. The single stripe and rating under the eagle on her sleeve is of an EM3 (electrician's mate, 3rd class). The tally on her cap, something that normally stated only "U.S. Navy," is of the USS *Texas*, a 1910 battleship that was refitted between the wars and designated the flagship of the US Atlantic Squadron in 1939. (approximately 5¼" x 8")

Figure 2-43. Wearing the uniform of her father—a US Navy chief petty officer (either a yeoman or gunner's mate; the image is not clear enough to discern)—Lill stands pigeon toed to emphasize his size 13 shoes on her considerably smaller feet.

A few post–World War II photos from around the world of women in men's uniforms can be found, though, as with the aftermath of the First World War, most had seen their fill of uniforms and wanted little to do with them after 1945. The genre reemerged during the 1960s in Germany for a brief period of time, mostly in Russian-occupied Deutsche Demokratische Republik (DDR, or East Germany), but this was a swiftly passing fad, rather than the reestablishment of an old trend. By the early 1970s, interest in the genre as a whole appears to have died out entirely.

Figure 2-44. This woman wears the dress blue uniform of her 1st Marine Division private first class husband, sans regulation trousers. The French *Fourragere*–the olive-green cord around her shoulder–was awarded to the 5th and 6th Marine Regiments by the French government for heroism at the Battle of Belleau Wood; to this day the regiments wear the *Fourragere*–the only ones authorized to do so–to honor those Marines.

Figures 3-1 and 3-2. In this rare photo, a woman wears an Afrika Korps uniform, hat, and boots of her sweetheart home from the war, if only temporarily. A vast number of combat veterans returned to the Reich on leave, and many took snapshots of their wives and girlfriends in uniform as keepsakes. Some photos are even inscribed, as the inset asks, whether one has ever seen so "sweet" (*süss*) a sight. ($2^{3}/_{8}$" x 3")

# 3

# Women of the Reich in Uniform

During World War II, the fad of photographing one's wife or girlfriend in uniform is confined almost entirely to Germany and those nations within its sphere of influence. The women of Italy and Germany's allies in the Balkans had little if any interest in the craze. As mentioned earlier, the trend was popular in France prior to occupation but failed to garner much interest in the British Isles and the United States. In all probability, this had more to do with how frequently *soldaten* returned home compared to their Allied counterparts.

All soldiers during the war earned roughly the same amount of leave in a year, but because Germany was centralized to the conflict, *soldaten* did not have nearly as far to travel to visit the homeland. More importantly, German soldiers had the resources to do so; trains ran regularly as part of the logistics of maintaining troops at the front, so the ability to travel to and from one's duty station was not difficult. As a result, although a number of photos were taken during the rise of the Third Reich in the 1930s, the majority were taken during the war itself, while *soldaten* were home on leave, as evidenced by the number in which combat badges and awards can be seen on the uniforms.

It was very different for Allied troops, who often had much-greater distances to travel to visit home, especially for those of the United States. American soldiers and airmen were stationed overseas for the duration and even after the war were not permitted to rotate home until they had fulfilled a strict point schedule. English soldiers in the European theater had roughly the same distance to travel as Germans did, but had no direct routes to do so. The resources for the Tommy to travel home and back for two to three weeks' leave simply were not available.

For the *frontovik* of the Soviet Union, leave was even more difficult. One could accumulate leave like any other soldier, but it was rarely granted. Unless one earned the right to be away from one's unit by acts of heroism or bravery, leave would be granted only once the conflict was over, often only for a few days at a time, and rarely far from the unit; the distances home from the front were simply too vast.

Figures 3-3 through 3-6. Sometimes the act of putting a woman into one's uniform could be as amusing as photos of the end result. Figure 3-6 (*bottom left*) shows the women in figures 3-94 through 3-96 preparing for their pictures. (reduced to roughly 75% of original size)

Figure 3-7. This Luftwaffe flak crewman prepares his lady for his souvenir, adjusting her collar and the marksmanship lanyard (more visible in figure 3-175). The back of the photo states, "Hans makes my tie in order."

For the most part, few dress uniforms such as the *Waffenrock* were worn; the majority of photos depict the various services' field uniforms, often complete with the equipment of war, even full packs and weapons (commonly worn home by vacationing *soldaten*).

The Heer (Army) is the most represented of the services. This is not surprising, since some 70% of all Germans in the military served in the Heer, as opposed to about 18% in the Luftwaffe (Air Force) and roughly 8% in the Kriegsmarine (Navy), though the Luftwaffe is overly represented for the percentage of those who served. This is primarily due to the fact that about half of Luftwaffe personnel were stationed within the Reich itself as defense against the Allied air offensive.

The least represented uniform is that of the Waffen-SS. Again, this is to be expected, since only 4 to 5% of the Wehrmacht were in the SS, so naturally fewer images would exist. Since images of the *SS* are more sought after by collectors, images of women wearing *SS* uniforms tend to cost considerably more than images represented by the other services, often by a factor of as much as ten.

Figures 3-8. A *soldat* adjusts the position of the rifle for this young girl, the niece of the housewife who served them, presumably in an occupied country. This photo was probably taken in 1943 or 1944, judging by the *einheitsfeldmütze* (unit field cap), which was not issued until later in the war.

Figure 3-9. The difficulty in collecting only photos of women wearing their husbands' uniforms is that one cannot always determine whether or not a woman is wearing her own uniform, especially after 1942. Increased bombing and the drain of manpower for the front brought many women into uniformed service. This woman could be wearing her own *kombi* (jumpsuit) or her husband's. (2½" x 3½")

In the majority of photos, the uniforms appear to fit the women rather well. No doubt some tucking and gathering of the uniform had to have taken place. Images do exist of women donning uniforms with their men assisting them, tugging the excess fabric of the tunic behind their backs into the belt, out of the shot. Some photos exist where the uniforms do not fit in the least, with tunic or coat cuffs all but swallowing ladies' hands and fingers, but fewer still exist of a woman wearing a uniform that does not close over her chest at all.

## Individuals

Most photos of women wearing men's uniforms are of a lone woman. Some of the pictures were shot indoors, but most were taken outside. Indoor photography often required the use of a flashbulb, provided they could be had, especially later in the war. If one was not skilled at reading a light meter or was easily confused by f-stops and shutter speeds, this had the potential to become a costly endeavor quite quickly. One is always better off using the sun instead of a flash.

For the most part, the subjects in these photos appear to be willing, if not thoroughly amused, participants. That is not to say they all smiled; there are some who imitated their *soldat*'s military bearing by standing at attention (or something close to it) with their eyes forward, chin jutted and high, or scowling. Others may have just been caught unawares as the shutter did its work, and admittedly, this appears to have been the situation in at least a few of the pictures shown. Yet, there are photographs of women who are not smiling, are not looking into the camera, or are otherwise disinterested in the photographer. There are also some who, although they might be smiling for the camera, seem as if their grins are insincere, and that there is somewhere else they would rather be.

Although there is almost certainly a degree of narcissism for those who agreed or volunteered to sit for the camera, there is quite possibly a sense of scopophobia for those who did not. The fear of being stared at, the opposite of scopophilia (more commonly known as voyeurism), and becoming the object, often sexual, of a voyeur's scrutiny can be understandably distressing. Knowing that a photograph would likely become an erotic talisman is enough to create apprehension, though this appears to be the exception and not the norm. As stated, the majority of these photos portray women who are as amused by wearing men's uniforms as their photographers. If there were women who had been coerced into posing, they seem to be few and far between.

Figures 3-10 through 3-15 (*following pages*):At the end of the Great War, Germany faced a great deal of civil unrest. In late 1919, the Weimar Republik assumed command of the nation and established the Vorläufiger Reichswehr (Temporary or Provisional National Defense), composed of the Reichsheer (National Army) and Reichsmarine (National Navy). The Reichsheer changed the uniform design to distinguish themselves from the Deutsche Freikorps (German Free Corps), a paramilitary organization of veterans who primarily wore their World War I uniforms and were decidedly less than civil themselves.

Figure 3-10 (*left*). This woman wears a Reichsheer uniform, though whether it is during the unrest following the Great War or later in the 1920s remains unknown. ($3^1/_2$" x $4^1/_2$")

Figure 3-11 (*right*). The woman wears a Reichsheer uniform from the 1920s, though she also wears what appears to be a National Socialist armband on her left sleeve. ($2^3/_4$" x $3^7/_8$")

Figure 3-12. Another woman wearing a Reichsheer uniform (note the absence of the party eagle from the cap), a winter coat (*mantel*), and a sidearm. Both the *mantel* and boots are far too large for her; the hem of the coat has been noticeably pinned up.

Figure 3-13. Taken between the end of the Great War and the late 1920s, this woman wears a Reichsmarine uniform.

Figures 3-14 and 3-15. (*above*) This photo of two women wearing Reichsmarine uniforms of the Weimar Republik was taken on July 10, 1932. (reverse side has been reduced)

Figures 3-17 and 3-18. On March 1, 1935, the Reichswehr was renamed the Wehrmacht and, in direct violation of the Treaty of Versailles, openly conscripted troops. Now answering to the Nazi Party, the regalia and symbolism of the party were added to the Reichswehr uniforms, as displayed here on the *waffenrock* (a dress uniform tunic) and *schirmmütze* (peaked cap) that these women wear.

Figures 3-16 and 3-19. (*right and bottom right previous*) Both of these women wear a *waffenrock* with the SA Sports Badge, positioned where the lower-left breast pocket would be. Instituted in 1933, the SA Sports Badge was a coveted fitness award that was authorized to be worn throughout the Wehrmacht and other uniformed services.

Figure 3-20. It is difficult to tell precisely whose tunic the woman is wearing, but the joviality of everyone in the photo is typical of this genre of photography. (3³/₈" x 4¹/₂")

Figure 3-21. This woman wears a *waffenrock* that is somewhat larger than she is. The sleeves almost entirely cover her hands, falling to her knuckles, and the trousers appear to have swallowed her feet. (2⁷/₈" x 4")

Figure 3-22. The sly smile on this woman (*right*) almost begs one to wonder whether she is struggling to keep a straight face, or if she is perhaps scheming some mischief above and beyond wearing someone's uniform. The lanyard draped from her right shoulder to her third button is an early version of the Heeres Schiessauszeichnung, the Army Marksmanship Award. (2³/₈" x 2⁷/₈")

Figures 3-23 through 3-25. A woman wears the *waffenrock* of a *gefreiter* (roughly equivalent to a lance or junior corporal) in these three photos–probably her son's. Note that in the image on the right, the insignia appears sewn on backward, and the sleeve chevron and Nazi eagle are reversed; this was a common problem when dealing with small negatives and prints that were sometimes accidentally reversed in the darkroom. ($2^{1}/_{2}$" x $3^{1}/_{2}$" each)

Figure 3-26. Judging by the length of the sleeves on the woman wearing this *waffenrock*, she appears to have a rather tall boyfriend. The ribbon on her left chest appears to be that of the Iron Cross.

Figure 3-27. This woman wears the *waffenrock* of an *unteroffizier* (noncommissioned officer) of some distinction. In addition to the *Schiessauszeichnung* lanyard, the uniform also bears the Heeres Dienstauszeichnung (Army Service Medal) and the DRL (Deutsches Reichsabzeichen für Leibesübungen) Sportabzeichen (German National Medal for Fitness).

Figure 3-28. This woman wears a *waffenrock* with an indeterminable medal and ribbon on her chest. The note on the back translates roughly to "He is in a hurry!"

Figures 3-29 and 3-30. Though very difficult to read, the reverse (reduced) of the photo of this woman in a *waffenrock* and *schirmmütze* translates (roughly) as "Dear Steffal, a dear girl who thinks she can pass for a soldier."

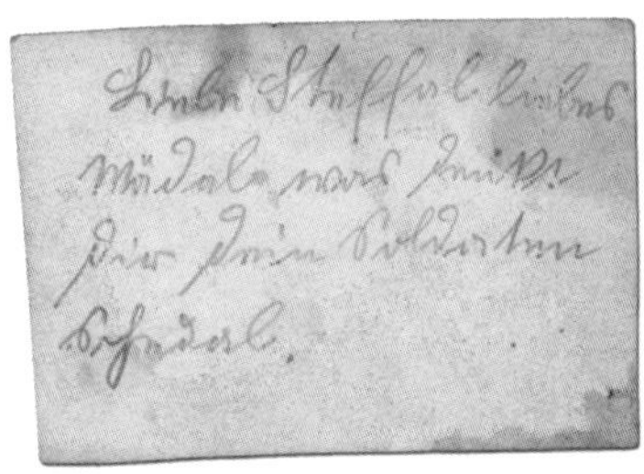

Figure 3-31. The woman in this photo is accompanied by what appears to be her sister. She wears the *waffenrock*, *schirmmütze*, and *tuchhosen* (trousers) of a *landser* (private).

Figure 3-32. The woman to the right wears her husband's complete uniform, which fits her rather well. (3³/₈" x 4³/₄")

Figure 3-33. The woman to the left wears her husband's *unteroffizier* uniform, hefting another item often associated with soldiers of all nations during the war: a cigarette. Even though the Nazis highly discouraged smoking for health reasons, many soldiers had few other ways to relieve the stress of combat. (2⁷/₈" x 4")

Figure 3-34. The woman on the right wears a *gefreiter*'s uniform of Infanterie Regiment 37 (the numbers of which are embroidered on the *schulterklappen*, or shoulder boards). Her bayonet bears a *portepee*, a knot reserved for segeants or others in positions of authority. (2⁵/₈" x 3⁵/₈")

Figure 3-35. This woman wears an officer's tunic, complete with cross belt and saber. In 90–95% of photos, women wear enlisted men's uniforms. not those of officers. (2³/₈" x 3¹/₂")

Figure 3-36. This woman salutes to the photographer from within her husband's *mantel* and *schirmmütze*. Her woolen stockings have been turned down over the top of his *schnürstiefel* (short boots). (2⁵/₈" x 3³/₄")

Figure 3-37. A young woman in her family kitchen wears a Wehrmacht uniform in this photo taken at an unusually artistic angle. (3¹/₄" x 4¹/₂")

Figure 3-38. The woman in this picture has opted to wear only her husband's *schirmmütze*, preferring to retain her own coat. (2¹/₂" x 3⁵/₈")

Figures 3-39 and 3-40. This woman wears her husband's cavalry officer's uniform and offers her son a ride. Figure 3-39 indicates that she appears to be an accomplished rider herself; most novices tend to put their entire foot in the stirrup, rather than just their toes. (2¹/₂" x 3⁷/₈" each)

Figures 3-42 and 3-43. Interestingly, it is not the wife who wears this *soldat*'s uniform, but either his sister or sister-in-law; the note on the back of the photo reads "The soldier and my bride."

Figure 3-44. This woman relaxes in her garden and wears her husband's *unteroffizier* uniform. Above the pocket and opposite the Wehrmacht eagle is what appears to be an Army Service Medal ribbon. (2³/₄" x 3⁷/₈")

Figure 3-41. The fancy striped caps at the top of the sleeves of this woman's *waffenrock* are normally reserved for military band members and musicians, a distinction that the Bundeswehr continues to use today. (2¹/₂" x 3¹/₄")

Figure 3-45. This "bride of a comrade," as noted on the back, wears her husband's oversized coat in the first of many winters of the war, in October 1939. It was not uncommon for *soldaten* to trade photographs of their family back home, including images of one another's wives and sweethearts. (3" x 4¹/₄")

Figure 3-46. A husband and wife share a chilly, uniformed moment together in October 21, 1940. (2$^{5}/_{8}$" x 3$^{3}/_{4}$")

Figure 3-47. This stern woman carries her husband's saber and wears a well-decorated *oberfähnrich's* uniform (an officer candidate from the senior sergeant's ranks) with the Iron Cross Second Class ribbon in the second button hole, Allgemeine Sturmabzeichen (General Assault Badge), and Verwundetenabzeichen im Schwarz (Wound Badge in Black).

Figures 3-48 and 3-49. This woman wears a Heer *mantel* and *feldmütze* (field cap), also known as a *schiffchen*, or "little ship." The back of the photo (reduced) is dated "*Kriegsjahr* [war year] 1939, 5 November."

Figures 3-50 through 3-52. Three different pictures taken at the same time but printed separately. The reverse of one photo states that the picture was taken in winter 1939, and another says winter 1939–40, so the one was probably printed after the first–whether shortly after they were taken or recently is unknown. Collectors must often be wary of less than reputable dealers, even when all else appears to be original. Thankfully this set was from an honest seller, and the original album indicates that the photo was printed in spring 1940. (each roughly $2^{1}/_{2}$" x $3^{5}/_{8}$")

Figure 3-53. Not all women who posed for photos in their husbands' uniforms were lithe beauties; this woman looks as if she was the one on active duty, rather than her husband. The legend on the reverse states "On true watch" in February 1940. ($2^{5}/_{8}$" x $3^{3}/_{4}$")

Figure 3-54. The woman above wears an *unteroffizier*'s uniform with the Ehrenkreuz des Weltkriegs (Cross of Honor of the World War) 1914/1918 ribbon with crossed swords, signifying that the uniform's owner was a frontline combat veteran of the Great War. ($2^{3}/_{8}$" x $3^{3}/_{4}$")

Figure 3-55. The woman in this *unteroffizier*'s uniform wears what looks like her husband's *dienstbrille* (service eye glasses), as well as his *feldmütze* and tunic. The uniform has the Schiessauszeichnung, an unknown ribbon, and what looks like the Wound Badge in Silver. ($2^{7}/_{8}$" x $4^{3}/_{4}$")

Figure 3-56. This woman (*right*) "reports" to her husband, a *gefreiter*. It is unfortunate the photo is black and white; if the picture was in color, the *waffenfarbe* (branch color) might have been determined: white denoted infantry; yellow, signals or reconnaissance; pink, armored, etc.

Figure 3-57. The reverse of this photo actually mentions the woman's name, Friedel, as well as that of her husband, Alfred. Taken in Wildau in 1940, in the southeastern outskirts of Berlin, Friedel relaxes with a cigarette in Alfred's *waffenrock*. ($3^{3}/_{4}$" x 5")

Figure 3-58. This woman wears a rather uncommon issue item with her husband's *schirmmütze*, a *kradmantel*. The rubberized double-breasted raincoat was popular with Heer officers (as shown), as well as motorcycle drivers and Kriegsmarine personnel. (4" x 5⁵/₈")

Figure 3-59. This jovial *soldat* salutes, her sleeves rolled into her cuffs and oversized trousers stuffed into the tops of her *marschstiefel* (marching boots). The back notes that the photo was taken in Brunn, just outside Regensburg, in 1940.

Figure 3-60. Wearing this sergeant's uniform, this woman sits within the crook of her bicycle. The cord dangling from her pocket above what appears to be the Bandenkampfabzeichen (Anti-Partisan Badge) is a *pfeifenschnur* (a whistle lanyard). The ribbon in her buttonhole is for the Iron Cross Second Class. ($2^3/_4$" x $3^7/_8$")

Figure 3-61. A different woman appears to be wearing the same uniform as in figure 3-60. Instead of a bicycle, she carries a cigarette, probably a favorite of the *soldat* who wore the uniform originally. (2⁵/₈" x 3⁵/₈")

Figure 3-62. The woman below, with her mother and sister, almost looks as if she has fallen asleep, though the shutter probably caught her as she was adjusting her posture. (2¹/₂" x 3³/₄")

Figure 3-63. The woman who wears this *gefreiter*'s *mantel*, boots, and *feldmütze* (*below*) appears amused at being photographed; the buildings in the background suggest that this might have been taken in Russia.

Figure 3-64. The woman on the left wears a *schirmmütze* and *mantel*. The civilian man who stands beside her could be her father or father-in-law.

Figures 3-65 and 3-66. Again, a rare occurrence in which a woman is named on the reverse of the photo (reduced): "Is she not lovely, is she not nice? Who then . . .? The young Miss Gerda." Gerda wears her *unteroffizier*'s uniform with the SA Sport Medal on the left pocket.

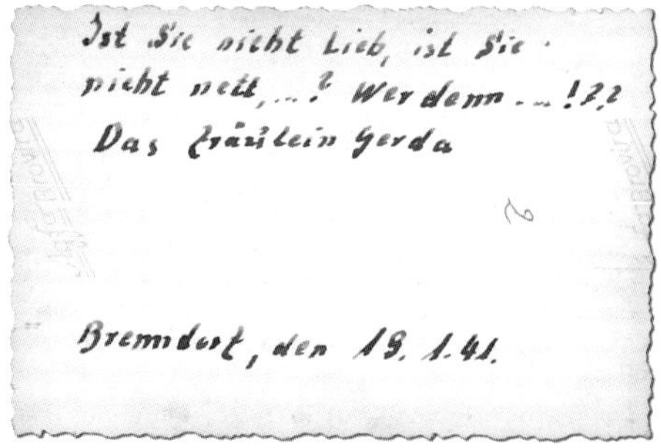


Figures 3-67 and 3-68. Taken moments apart and in the winter months, the woman in these photos has thought better of waiting for her husband and has donned his *mantel*, belt, and saber for the second picture. ($2^1/_2$" x $3^3/_4$" each)

Figure 3-69. The six *soldaten* in this photo seem far more amenable to accompany their companion than she appears. It is difficult to tell whether this picture was taken in Germany or one of the occupied countries, which could explain the woman's lack of enthusiasm.

Figure 3-70. The woman below strikes a cavalier posture in her husband's *mantel*, boots, and *feldmütze* in the snows outside their home. ($2^5/_8$" x $3^7/_8$")

Figure 3-71. Posing in warmer months, this woman seems quite happy to pose in her "acquired" Heer uniform. This photo illustrates how the parallax angle of viewfinder cameras can often affect the composition of a photo.

Figure 3-72. This woman wears what appears to be her father's uniform; the medals on her chest are the 1914 Iron Cross and the Cross of Honor of the World War. (2 3/8" x 3 1/2")

Figure 3-73. Sandwiched between two admiring *soldaten*, this woman does not seem to mind the attention. (3" x 4")

Figure 3-74. This woman wears her husband's *mantel* and *feldmütze*, and carries his *handschuen* (gloves). The photo was taken in the chill of late winter or early spring; fallen leaves would be visible if it was taken in autumn. (2 3/8" x 3 5/8")

Figure 3-75. The young Yugoslavian woman wearing the *gefreiter*'s uniform in this picture appears much more amused than her watchful relative (mother?) on the bench behind her. (2 1/2" x 3 5/8")

Figure 3-76. This charming young lady wears a *gefreiter*'s uniform amid a stand of small pines. (2 1/2" x 3 1/2")

Figure 3-77. This surly-looking woman, who appears to be struggling to keep a straight face, wears a Heer *landser*'s (private's) uniform with a Wound Badge in Black just visible at the base of her left pocket. (2⅝" x 3¾")

Figure 3-78. This *panzerjäger* and his wife pose on their doorstep. The silver "P" on his epaulett, along with what could well be pink trim, indicates the *soldat*'s service.

Figure 3-79. This woman stands in ankle-deep snow for a picture in her husband's uniform. Unlike the woman in figure 3-55, the glasses she wears appear to be her own. (2⅝" x 3⅞")

Figure 3-80. The patch on this woman's right cuff, and presumably his as well, indicates that the *soldat* is a *sanitäter* (medic). He also has the Wound Badge in Black on his left pocket. (2⅞" x 3⅝")

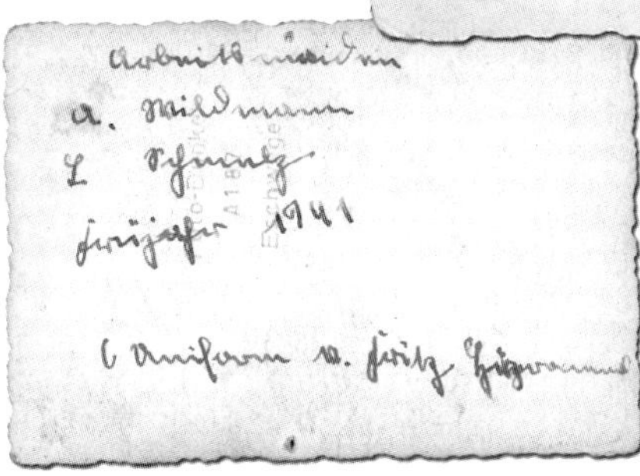

Figures 3-81 through 3-84. The same photograph was printed on two separate occasions (indicated by the different batch numbers on the back) and shared among comrades. The picture was taken in spring 1941 (Frühjahr 1941) of *arbeitsmaiden* (work maids) Annemarie Wildman and Luise Schmetz. The back of the first photo also notes that the uniform belonged to Fritz Hügrammund (?).

Figure 3-85. Because of fabric restrictions during the war, many brides in a number of different countries were forced to forgo wedding dresses, but the bouquet was always present. In this "wedding portrait," it is not certain whether the woman in uniform is standing in for the *soldat*, or whether she is the actual bride-to-be. The small hook at the bottom of the belt is part of an internal support system of the *feldbluse* that helped spread the weight of a *soldat*'s equipment.

Figure 3-86. This picture was shot on a square-format box camera, such as an Agfa Box 44, and printed on rectangular paper to facilitate holding the photo without risking fingerprints on the image itself.

Figure 3-87. This woman poses in her *landser*'s uniform on a windy day. Her *schulterklappen* (shoulder boards) each have a sleeve slipped over them; many times these had regimental numbers embroidered on them, but the ones in this photo do not appear to have any such markings.

Figure 3-88. Although it appears as if this was a studio portrait, the photo to the right is a homemade snapshot of a woman in an *unteroffizier*'s uniform and *schirmmütze* with printed cloth or drapery behind her. ($3^1/_2$" x $5^1/_2$")

Figure 3-89. This gallantly posing woman wears her *gefreiter*'s *mantel* and *schirmmütze*, but her own boots, complete with zipper closure on the front.

Figure 3-90. The woman wearing this *mantel* is considerably smaller than its original owner; the sleeves have all but swallowed her hands. ($2^1/_2$" x $3^5/_8$")

Figure 3-91. This woman is quite literally out standing in her field. She wears an *unteroffizier*'s uniform with *schiessauszeichnung* marksmanship lanyard and Wound Badge in Black on her pocket. (3" x $4^{7}/_{8}$")

Figure 3-92. This woman seems ready for combat, wearing a *landser*'s tunic over her checked apron and flowered dress and a *stahlhelm* (helmet), but also a belt with cartridge boxes, even standing ready with a K98k Mauser rifle and bayonet. The military caisson and bulging pockets of the tunic lead one to believe that the picture was taken on the march.

Figures 3-93 and 3-94. This photo is an original reproduction. Film captured by the Russians during the war was printed and stored in archives, so the print is not originally German, but dates to 1945 or, in some cases, even earlier. The "pogasheno" stamp indicates this photo has been officially withdrawn. This *leutnant*'s wife wears his uniform with an officer's aiguillette and dress dagger. ($3^{3}/_{8}$" x $4^{3}/_{4}$")

Figures 3-94 through 3-96. These three women from figure 3-6 each pose for their separate photographs in the family garden. They have taken turns wearing the same *unteroffizier*'s uniform with the Iron Cross Second Class ribbon.

Figure 3-97. Not all women who wore a *soldat*'s uniform were German. These men of Infanterie Regiment 4, smitten by a local Frenchwoman, have adorned her with a *schirmmütze*, though she seems less than pleased by the attention.

Figure 3-98. This woman wears a Model 1940 *feldbluse*; the hook for the internal harness is plainly visible on her belt. The dark *waffenfarbe* (service color) could denote an assignment to either medical, combat engineer, or veterinary service. Without knowing the precise color or seeing a specialist's patch, it is difficult to say for sure.

Figure 3-99. Armed with a charming smile, this woman also wears a Model 1940 *feldbluse* (field tunic) and *schirmmütze*.

Figure 3-100. Wearing what appears to be a Model 1940 tunic with Model 1936 *unteroffizier* shoulder boards, this woman perches on a tall picnic table in the backyard of their home. (2 5/8" x 3 3/4")

Figure 3-101. The woman wearing this *obergefreiter's* uniform appears concerned. Did the photographer catch her unawares, or perhaps in midsentence?

Figure 3-102. Although most women wore uniforms of their loved ones that were too large for them, not all women were smaller than their beloved *soldat.* This rather full-figured woman wears a Model 1940 *feldbluse* of a considerably thinner man and carries his bayonet much like a diminutive saber. (3½" x 5½")

Figure 3-103. The owner of this woman's uniform must have recently returned from Russia; she wears a Model 1940 *feldbluse* that has an ostmedaille (eastern front medal) ribbon in the second button hole, winter trigger mittens, and early-model *filzstiefel* (felt boots) typical of what was issued on the eastern front.

Figure 3-104. This young lady appears to be less than enthused about wearing the Model 1936 uniform and *schirmmütze*, as if she wishes the photographer would just hurry up and get it over with.

Figure 3-105. If only photographs could speak; this woman wears a German *schirmmütze* but an open-collared French army tunic. No doubt there was a very interesting tale behind this picture. (3" x 3³/₄")

Figure 3-106. (*left*) This woman wears a *schirmmütze* and a *gefreiter*'s Model 1940 uniform with the Iron Cross ribbon in the button hole. The *schulterklappen* are edged with what has to be white *waffenfarbe* trim, signifying infantry. (2 1/2" x 3 1/2")

Figure 3-107. This woman stands beside her boyfriend, an *obergefreiter* who has earned the Infanterie Sturmabzeichen (Infantry Assault Badge). Barely visible below and to the left of that badge is the Wound Badge in Black. (2 1/2" x 3 5/8")

Figure 3-108 (*left*). Looking almost as if they had traded uniforms, this woman wears a Model 1940 uniform that is actually the same size as that worn by the *soldat* to the left; it appears smaller only because she is so much shorter than he is. Precisely what he is wearing on his feet is an entirely different story. (2 1/2" x 3 1/2")

Figure 3-109. This woman wears a Model 1940 *gefreiter*'s uniform, along with her beau's *feldmütze*. Note that this variant has painted buttons, rather than the silver buttons common on previous uniforms. (2 5/8" x 3 5/8")

Figures 3-110 and 3-111. These two pictures are of a woman wearing an *oberschütze's* (senior, literally "over," private) model 1940 *feldbluse*; the rank is indicated by the diamond-like patch on her sleeve. *oberschütze* (also *oberkannonier*, senior cannoneer), and *obergrenadier* (senior grenadier), etc. was honorific; it recognized aptitude for those who would not likely qualify for *gefreiter*. Note the *pfeifenschnur* in the right breast pocket.

Figure 3-112. Two stripes on the cuff of a *soldat*'s sleeve signified that the sergeant was the *hauptfeldwebel*, or primary sergeant, nicknamed "Spiess" (spear). It wasn't a rank, but a position, and any noncommissioned officer could be appointed. This barefooted woman wears the model 1940 *feldbluse* of an *oberfeldwebel*–roughly equivalent to a US Army master sergeant–who had been awarded the Iron Cross Second Class and the General Assault Badge. (2$^{5}/_{8}$" x 3$^{3}/_{4}$")

Figures 3-113 and 3-114. One of the permissible reasons for *soldaten* to go on leave was to return home to assist with the harvest. (One of the primary causes of food shortages in the Great War had been the drain of manpower from the farms to the front.) These photos, though of different women, are in similar settings, but could just as easily have been Russian girlfriends.

Figure 3-115. The woman in this photo appears to be quite amused by her surroundings. She wears a Model 1936 *feldbluse*, *marschstiefel*, and belt with *patronenkiste* (cartridge box). Around her neck, as well as on several *soldaten* behind her, are a pair of goggles typical of those worn by motorcycle troops and *panzergrenadieren* (armored infantry). The *stahlhelm* has a large rubber band (often cut from a discarded inner tube) to hold camouflage in place. The photo was taken in Treuenbrietzen, where over 1,000 residents were executed by the Red Army in May 1945.

Figure 3-116. The uniform this woman wears is a simple model 1940 *feldbluse*, while her *soldat* (*right*) has opted to wear a suit for the picture with two Winterhilfswerk (Winter Assistance) pins in his lapel. The Winterhilfswerk (WHW) was a social welfare organization that offered the pins in exchange for donations. ($2^{1}/_{2}$" x $3^{5}/_{8}$")

Figure 3-117. This woman seems weighed down by all the gear she is wearing: a K98k rifle, belt, and cartridge boxes, and even a full Tornister field pack. She wears a model 43 *feldbluse* and *Einheitsfeldmütze*. The dark blotch in the foreground is the shadow of the photographer.

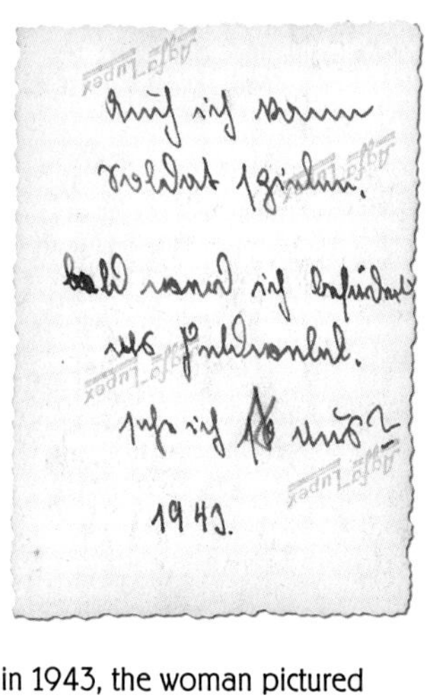


Figures 3-118 and 3-119. Probably mailed to the *soldat* in this photo in 1943, the woman pictured has added the caption on the reverse, "I too can play the *soldat*." (Reverse has been reduced)

Figures 3-120. The woman to the left wears this *oberfeldwebel*'s spiess uniform, adorned with the Iron Cross Second Class ribbon and what appears to be a chocolate bar tucked into the tunic below it. The photo was taken in Büsseldorf (near Bad Neuenahr) in 1943.

Figure 3-121. This saluting woman wears a *gefreiter*'s model 1943 *feldbluse* that has had the collar replaced with darker material (a common tailor's modification). She wears a field cap, or *einheitsfeldmütze*, a cap modeled after the earlier *bergmütze* of the mountain troops or *gebirgsjäger*. The badge on her pocket is the Wound Badge in Black.

Figure 3-122. This jovial woman wears the uniform of her *oberschütze*.

Figure 3-123. The woman to the right wears the uniform of a rather decorated *soldat*; her model 1940 *feldbluse* with modified collar bears the Iron Cross Second Class ribbon, an Ostfrontmedaille (Eastern Front Medal) ribbon, an Infantry Assault Badge, and what appears to be a Wound Badge in Gold, a very rare badge that was awarded only after a *soldat* suffered five or more wounds.

Figure 3-124. Taken in 1943 according to the date at the bottom, this shows a woman relaxing in an officer's uniform (probably a *leutnant*). The badges on the pocket include the Wound Badge in Black and the Panzerkampfabzeichen, or Tank Assault (Battle) Badge. The poor quality of the photo makes it difficult to identify the two ribbons above the pocket.

Figure 3-125. This woman wears an *obergefreiter*'s highly decorated model 1940 *feldbluse* and an *einheitsfeldmütze*. The owner, a *sanitäter* (field medic; note the patch on the right sleeve), has been awarded the Iron Cross Second Class, a Wound Badge in Black, the Infantry Assault Badge, and an SA Sport Medal.

Figure 3-126. It is not certain whether this woman was caught talking or yawning, but she wears a *gefreiter's mantel* (overcoat) and *einheitsfeldmütze* with an earlier style of Wehrmacht eagle and cockade. ($2^7/_8$" x 4")

Figure 3-126A. These three smiling women wear the model 1943 *feldbluse* and *einheitsfeldmütze*. The woman on the left has a Wound Badge in Black on her pocket.

Figures 3-127 through 3-131. Tank crewmen were issued a specific uniform in addition to their *feldbluse*, the *panzerjacke* (tank jacket). Issued in black (to help hide the grime that often coated armored crews), the *panzerjacke* was also issued in *feldgrau* (field gray) to *panzerjäger* (anti-tank personnel, literally "tank hunter") and Sturmgeschütz self-propelled artillery troops who crewed armored vehicles.

Figure 3-127. This woman wears an early panzer officer's uniform and belt with the model 1934 *schutzmütze* (protective cap). Impractical with radio head sets, the *schutzmütze* was discontinued in 1941.

Figure 3-128. The *panzerjacke* was piped in pink to indicate tank crewmen. It is not often discernible in black-and-white photos, but it stands out here on this *gefreiter*'s uniform with the Tank Assault Badge.

Figure 3-129. This woman's black dress almost makes it look like she is wearing a *panzerjacke* dress.

Figure 3-130. As the war progressed, certain details were eliminated to simplify production due to shortages of material. This *panzerjacke* has no piping on the collar; this third pattern was issued later in the war.

Figure 3-131. As mentioned, not all *panzerjacken* were issued in black. This woman wears a *panzerjäger*'s uniform; the *waffenfarbe* appears to be pink, not red, which would appear much darker in a black-and-white photo and would indicate a *Sturmgeschütz* crew classified as artillery.

Figure 3-132. This woman wears her husband's *matrosenfeldwebel* (chief petty officer) uniform and *schirmmütze*. She salutes her honor guard of Kriegsmarine *matrosen* (sailors) in their summer uniforms as her husband returns the honor from the near end of the line. (3³/₈" x 4⁷/₈")

Figure 3-133. As with many navies, uniforms were quite versatile. The summer uniform could be a mix of white *matrosenhemden* (sailor's shirts) with blue trousers, white trousers, or even a blue *matrosenjacke* (sailor's jacket), such as what this woman wears.

Figure 3-134. The woman to the right wears a winter variant of the Kriegsmarine summer uniform above. (The shirt she wears is her own.) The tally on her *tellermütze* (flat cap) reads "Kreuzer Emden," indicating that her loved one was a *matrosenobergefreiter* (literally Navy over-corporal) on the cruiser *Emden*. (3" x 5")

Figure 3-135. This couple each wear the *zimmermansmaat* (carpenters mate) uniform for the *schnellbootflotilla* (fast boat flotilla). The S-boot, or E-boat as the British called them, were the Kriegsmarine equivalent of American PT boats, carrying multiple torpedoes and relying on speed for defense. This photo was taken on June 21, 1936, in Rissen, on the outskirts of Hamburg.

Figure 3-136. This smiling woman wears a Kriegsmarine summer uniform that provides excellent camouflage against the winter snows of her yard. The rating patch on her left sleeve appears be a fire control rating for a gunner.

Figure 3-137. This *matrosengefreiter* (Navy corporal) and his family pose in his winter uniform. The woman is wearing an *überzieher*, or peacoat, a traditional navy overcoat. Unfortunately, the tally on her (his) *tellermütze* is illegible.

Figures 3-138 and 3-139. The woman in the *überzieher* in these two photos wears a winter uniform and *tellermütze* bearing only the word "Kriegsmarine." This is not unusual, since not every vessel or detachment had its own unique ribbon.

Figure 3-140. Wearing the uniform of her *obermaat artillerie mechaniker* (senior ordnance engineer's mate), this woman strikes a valiant pose for her photographer. ($2^{1}/_{4}$" x $2^{3}/_{4}$")

Figures 3-141 through 3-143. These three women each wear the *tellermütze* and *überzieher* peacoat. The collar insignia indicate the lower *mannschaften* (enlisted) ranks, though only the woman in figure 3-143 wears a coat with a rating visible, that of a *steuermannsmaat* (coxswain's mate) *matrosengefreiter.*

Figure 3-144. This *matrose* and girlfriend pose for the camera while he was home on leave in March 1941. She wears his Kriegsmarine *tellermütze*. ($2^3/_8$" x $3^1/_2$")

Figure 3-145. This large photo (*left*) shows a woman wearing the *überzieher* of another *bootsmanns* (boatswain) *matrosenobergefreiter*. The badge on her coat is the Kriegsabzeichen für Minensuchverbände, the Wartime Minesweeper Badge. As she poses, a child, presumably a younger sibling, peers on from the window behind her. ($3^5/_8$" x $5^1/_2$")

Figure 3-146. A woman wears a winter sailor's jumper. The Kriegsmarine *tellermütze* drooping across her eyes appears to be several sizes larger than she is accustomed to wearing.

Figures 3-147 and 3-148. Two photos of the same woman clad in the *überzieher* of a *bootsmann matrosenobergefreiter.* ($2^5/_8$" x $3^7/_8$" each)

Figures 3-149 and 3-150. Another woman–identified as "a sailor girl" and taken in October 1943–wearing an *überzieher* with the Minesweeper Badge. If it is the same *matrose* whose uniform is shown in figure 3-145; he has been promoted to *bootsmannsmaat,* indicated by the collar insignia. (The reverse has been reduced.)

Figures 3-151 and 3-152. Identified as Heide Schwarz, the woman in the checked dress trades identifying as a sailor with her friend. Once again wearing the *überzieher* of a *bootsmann matrosenobergefreiter* with the Minesweeper Badge, though now adding an Iron Cross Second Class ribbon, these women had their picture taken on March 21, 1945.

Figure 3-153. This woman doesn't appear to have her sea legs. She wears an *überzieher* with both *bootsmann matrosenobergefreiter* patches on her sleeve and a Minesweeper Badge similar to that in figure 3-161. It is not the same woman; could it be the same sailor? (3" x 4$^7/_8$")

Figure 3-154. In direct violation of the Treaty of Versailles, Germany established the Luftwaffe on February 26, 1935. This woman wears an early *stabgefreiter's tuchrock* (service tunic) with an airman's Schiessauszeichnung (Marksmanship award). (2 1/2" x 3 5/8")

Figure 3-155. Although the clothing and equipment this woman wears appears to be that of a Heer uniform, it is actually a Luftwaffe uniform. The photo is too dark to make out many details, but the Luftwaffe belt buckle is clear enough to distinguish. (3 3/8" x 5 3/8")

Figure 3-156. These two women play at wooing the *soldat*, a Luftwaffe *feldwebel* (roughly equivalent to a US Army staff sergeant) with *mantel*, *schirmmütze*, and dagger falls victim to "his" love. (2 1/2" x 3 5/8")

Figure 3-157. This woman also wears a Luftwaffe *feldwebel*'s uniform of *fliegerbluse*, *schirmmütze*, and belt, though at a warmer time of year. (2½" x 3⅝")

Figure 3-158. For the most part, the cover of the *schirmmütze* was often the same *feldblau* (field blue) of the Luftwaffe uniform, but a white lightweight cover for summer was also authorized.

Figure 3-159. A prewar photo of a highly amused woman wearing a Luftwaffe *flieger*'s coat and *schirmmütze* astride a Puch S4 motorcycle. (2⅝" x 3¾")

Figure 3-160. It is difficult to tell whether the *waffenfarbe* on this uniform is yellow (flight) or white (Hermann Göring Division), but this woman wears a Luftwaffe *unteroffizier*'s uniform with *schiessauszeichnung*. One wonders whether the *soldat* to the left in the Heer uniform is an in-law. (2½" x 3⅝")

Figure 3-161. The back of this photo reads, "For you, my darling, your little flak soldier." What looks like a large badge on the woman's Luftwaffe *mantel* is actually a drop of developer that splashed onto the photo after it had been rinsed. (3³/₄" x 5¹/₂")

Figure 3-162. A family gathered for this photo at what appears to be a *biergarten* (beer garden) in which a woman wears a Luftwaffe *schirmmütze* with a white summer cover, rather than the typical *feldblau* (field blue) woolen cover.

Figures 3-163. This woman wears the more common Luftwaffe *schirmmütze* with the wool cover. The reverse reads, "My brave little soldier-girl."

Figures 3-164 through 3-166. These women in Luftwaffe uniforms pose on a civilian motorcycle from Westfalen (Westphalia), indicated by the "IX" code on the license plate. The cycle was made by NSU Motorenwerke, the same company that made the Kettenkrad, a military half-tracked motorcycle. The woman on the back seat in figure 3-174 who wears an *oberleutnant*'s (First Lieutenant) uniform receives a Luftwaffe *unteroffizier* on the front porch. More shenanigans by the same individuals can be seen in figures 3-315 and 3-316.

Figure 3-167. This woman wears what may be considered a rather plain *flieger*'s (airman) uniform. It may be unadorned, but it was the hard-working *flieger* who kept the Luftwaffe in the air and Allied bombers at bay.

Figure 3-168. This woman wears a Luftwaffe *feldwebel*'s uniform that obviously belongs to a much taller individual.

Figure 3-169. This woman's *untefeldwebel*'s uniform fits her quite well, almost as if it was her own. Women in Luftwaffe service were issued a uniform akin to the *fliegerbluse*, but were never issued the men's *schirmmütze*.

Figure 3-170. This woman seems less than enthused about wearing a uniform, especially one that fits her so loosely.

Figure 3-171. At times, the photos of a woman wearing a man's clothing can provide intimate details about their relationship. This woman wears a Luftwaffe *schirmmütze*, but also men's pajamas. Was she wearing someone's cap and hospital clothing, or had this picture been taken following a particularly romantic moment at home?

Figure 3-172. This woman wears a Luftwaffe *unteroffizier*'s uniform, but no awards or other insignia adorn it.

Figures 3-173 and 3-174. The portraits of this woman are interesting; she wears a Luftwaffe *fliegerbluse* and *schirmmütze* but also wears a Winterhilfswerk (Winter Assistance) charitable donation pin, a stylized Germanic axe. (approximately $2\frac{1}{4}$" x $2\frac{1}{2}$" each)

Figures 3-175 and 3-176. The back of this photo says it all: "Good disposition." The woman wearing this full Luftwaffe *obergefreiter*'s uniform with *sportabzeichen*, *schiessauszeichnung*, and flak insignia (*left cuff*) is the same woman pictured preparing for this photo in figure 3-7.

Figure 3-177. These two women (*above*), one wearing a Luftwaffe *gefreiter*'s uniform and *schiffchen* and the other a Dirndl-style dress, are in all likelihood related, either to each other or the owner of the uniform.

Figure 3-178. Saluting from her picnic setting and in her stocking feet, this woman wears a Luftwaffe *obergefreiter*'s *fliegerbluse* and *schirmmütze*.

Figures 3-179 and 3-180. These two photos include a woman wearing a Luftwaffe *unteroffizier*'s *fliegerbluse* and *schirmmütze* while accompanied by a rather indifferent family cat. Interestingly, the *fliegerbluse* does not have the Luftwaffe eagle on the right breast. ($2^5/_8$" x $3^7/_8$")

Figure 3-181. The women above, one of whom wears the *fliegerbluse* and *schiffchen* of an *unteroffizier* in a flak (field division?) regiment, appear to be posing for two photographers, only one of whom has their attention.

Figure 3-182. This woman in the *feldwebel*'s uniform and wearing the stern visage also has the Luftwaffe NCO dagger and *portepee*. ($2^1/_2$" x $3^5/_8$")

Figure 3-183. The woman pictured on the previous page with her cat is shown here wearing a Luftwaffe overcoat (*mantel*) over her uniform. True to form, the cat in the previous images has deigned not to join her. ($2^5/_8$" x $3^7/_8$")

Figure 3-184. In a rare photograph of the uniform of a specific unit, the woman above wears a *tuchrock* of the Hermann Göring Division, indicated by the white collar insignia and the barely discernible cuff title on her right arm. The ribbons on her left chest are difficult to see but appear to be the service medal and the Iron Cross. ($2^3/_8$" x $3^1/_2$")

Figure 3-185. The Luftwaffe *flieger's tuchrock* in this photo has a single ribbon above the left pocket, though it is difficult to tell which one. The woman wears it over a rather stylish dress (note the collar) and *schiffchen.*

Figure 3-186. This woman salutes while she wears an *obergefreiter's fliegerbluse* and a *schirmmütze* that has been cocked at a jaunty angle. The insignia on the left cuff is that of a flak crewman, verified by the Flak-Kampfabzeichen (Anti-Aircraft Battle medal) on the lower left breast. (2 1/2" x 3 5/8")

Figure 3-187. The same woman from the previous figure poses for a second photo, though she appears to either be losing interest or getting cold.

Figure 3-188. This couple appears to be enjoying a picnic in the countryside; the wrappers of their lunch sit behind the *feldwebel*'s right leg. He wears a Luftwaffe-issued pullover (sweater), and she her woolen socks, leading one to believe that he may have given her his *fliegerbluse* to ward off a chill.

Figure 3-189. A mother wears her husband's oversized *tuchrock* and *schirmmütze* while she holds their son, who is more interested in a postcard than the photographer.

Figures 3-190 and 3-191. At first glance, one might think someone had sewn her husband's uniform insignia on incorrectly, but the negative was reversed when this print was made. On the back she asks, "How do I look as an airman?," and signs it, "Deine Kameradin," or "your female comrade." (Back has been reduced.)

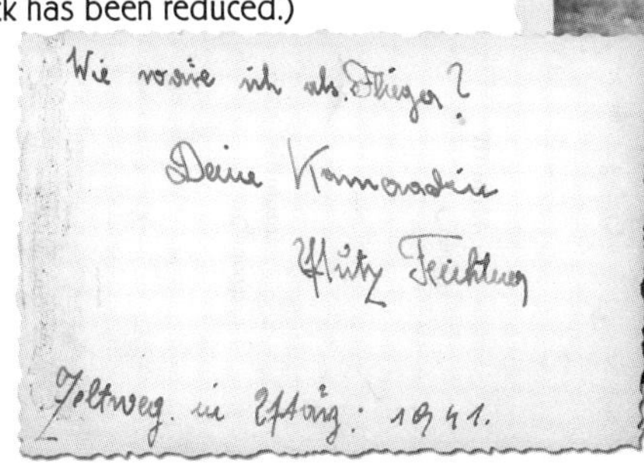

Figure 3-192. This atypically large snapshot of a woman wearing a *fliegerbluse* and *schirmmütze* was taken in a bedroom; note the frame of the bed in the background. (3³/₄" x 5⁷/₈")

Figure 3-193. This woman wears an *unteroffizier*'s *tuchrock* and *tuchhosen* (service trousers), but what appears to be her own *schiffchen*, though of which service is difficult to determine. (2⁵/₈" x 3¹/₂")

Figure 3-194. This *unteroffizier*'s *fliegerbluse* seems out of place; the medal on the left pocket is the Luftwaffe Fallschirmschützenabzeichen (Paratrooper Badge), but the *waffenfarbe* is not yellow, the color reserved for paratroopers. Again, difficult to tell in a black-and-white photo, the *kragenspiegel* (collar insignia) appear to be red, signifying an artillerist, but could just as easily be dark green (admin) or dark blue (medical).

Figures 3-195 through 3-197. These three women–two daughters and their mother–wear the same *unteroffizier's fliegerbluse* and *schiffchen*. All three seem quite happy to have daddy home. (approximately $2^3/_8$" x $3^1/_2$" each)

Figure 3-198. The woman in this heavily scratched photo poses with her family while wearing a Luftwaffe *gefreiter's fliegerbluse* and *schiffchen*. ($2^1/_2$" x $3^3/_4$")

Figure 3-199. The woman here seems more than happy to pose in a *gefreiter's* uniform while striking a relaxed pose that she probably learned from her boyfriend.

Figures 3-200 and 3-201. Displaying a number of toys and souvenirs from a festival of some sort, this woman smiles while wearing her beau's *obergefreiter*'s *fliegerbluse*. The caption on the reverse reads, "Is that not sweet?"

Figure 3-202. A woman overlooks the snow-covered fields of her home while wearing an *unteroffizier*'s *mantel* (overcoat) and *schiffchen*. ($2\frac{3}{4}$" x $3\frac{3}{8}$")

Figure 3-203. Two women pose as soldier and lover.

Figure 3-204. The insignia on the cuff of the *gefreiter*'s uniform indicate its owner serves in a flak regiment. The medal on her left chest is the SA Sportabzeichen.

Figure 3-205. This enthusiastic woman salutes while wearing an *obergefreiter*'s *fliegerbluse*, *schiffchen* and, visible just below the hem of her dress, her *mann*'s *marschstiefel* (marching or "jack" boots). ($3^{1}/_{8}$" x $4^{1}/_{2}$")

Figure 3-206. The woman to the left wears the *fliegerbluse* of a young combat veteran (the rank insignia is only that of a *flieger*); the ribbon at the button hole is the Iron Cross Second Class, and the medal above her left arm is the Erdkampfabzeichen der Luftwaffe (Ground Assault Badge).

Figure 3-207. The woman wearing this Luftwaffe *tuchrock* has been seen before, though wearing a Wehrmacht *feldbluse* (see figure 3-104). She appears to be equally enthusiastic.

Figure 3-208. Not all *soldaten* were youthful conscripts; many had served in the Great War. As a result, not all wives were young. This woman wears a Luftwaffe *unteroffizier*'s uniform with what appears to be the Hanseatenkreuz (Hansa City Cross) of Hamburg, a First World War award for bravery to men from the medieval cities of Hamburg, Lübeck, and Bremen. (2 1/2" x 3 1/2")

Figures 3-209 and 3-210. These Bavarian women pose at a street sign on the way to Astheim, some 15 miles east of Würzburg. One woman wears the *fliegerbluse* of an *unteroffizier* across her shoulders and over her Bavarian-style jacket; one can see the typical decorations on her lapels. The uniform is adorned with both the Iron Cross First Class and the Fallschirmschützenabzeichen. The third medal, to the right of the Paratrooper Badge, cannot be clearly identified.

Figure 3-211. Scanned from a negative, this image (*below*) of a woman saluting has been enhanced for clarity. She wears a white summer *schirmmütze* and a *flieger*'s *tuchrock*; there is a technician's badge on the left cuff that appears to be the Flugzeuggerät Tätigkeitsabzeichen (aircraft equipment occupation badge).

Figure 3-212. A woman wears a *gefreiter*'s *fliegerbluse* with a *bergmütze* (mountain cap, predecessor to the more common M-43 *einheitsfeldmütze*). The owner of the uniform was probably aircrew or a young pilot, since the badge on the left chest is the NSFK (Nationalsozialistische Flieger Korps) *Segelfliegerabzeichen*, National Socialist Flying Corps Glider Pilot Badge. The two gulls indicate a 60-second solo flight with a complicated maneuver.

Figure 3-213. The woman leaning out of the window in this staged snapshot also wears a Luftwaffe *bergmütze* (mountain cap). The *bergmütze* had only one button holding the ear flaps up; the *einheitsfeldmütze* had two.

Figure 3-214. This woman wears the *tuchrock* and *schirmmütze* of a vehicle driver, indicated by the Kraftfahrpersonal (motor vehicle personnel) specialty badge on the cuff. The Deutsches Schutzwall-Ehrenzeichen, better known to collectors as the Atlantic Wall Medal, hangs from the left pocket alongside a Winterhilfswerk donation pin (a miniature dagger).

Figures 3-215 through 3-217. As the war dragged on, more and more women were first encouraged and then required to enter military service, particularly in the Luftwaffe flak service. As a result, it is often difficult with mid- to late-war photographs to know whether women are wearing their own uniforms or those of their loved ones. In this case, the inscription on the back of figure 3-226 from February 8, 1945, is a "pretty souvenir of Frau Varsel (?) and Anni," a likely indicator that they are Luftwaffe servicewomen, much like the woman in the *mantel* to the left. (Figure 3-215 is shown at full size; figures 3-216 and 3-217 are $3\frac{3}{4}$" x $5\frac{5}{8}$")

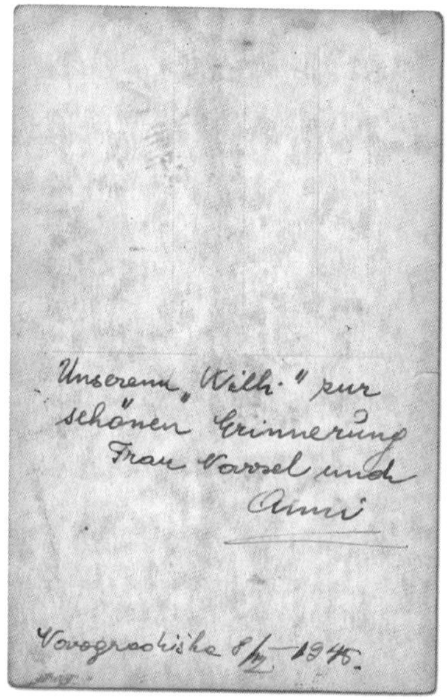

Figures 3-218 through 3-221. Photographs of Waffen SS personnel are much more rare than that of the Heer or Luftwaffe, primarily because fewer men served in the SS. As a result, photos of women wearing a man's Waffen SS uniform are also more. The two snapshots (*above*) both show a woman wearing an *SS-sturmmann* (roughly equivalent to a lance corporal) uniform, complete with Iron Cross Second Class ribbon and what appears to be the Infanterie-Sturmabzeichen (Infantry Assault Badge). In the images below, one woman wears an *SS-oberscharführer*'s (equivalent to a US Army staff sergeant) uniform with Iron Cross Second Class ribbon, while her female accomplice wears a man's suit and fedora. (Photo on right reduced.)

Figures 3-222 through 3-224. The Party created a number of paramilitary and civilian services, most of whom wore distinct uniforms. From the Sturmabteilung (SA or Storm Troopers) to political services, women whose uniformed husbands served on the home front had their pictures taken in uniform as well, as shown in these photos. For instance, the woman in the center image wears a uniform of the Deutsche Arbeitsfront (German Work Front, a labor service). ($2\frac{3}{8}$" x $3\frac{5}{8}$" each)

Figures 3-225 through 3-227. All German males were required to serve for six months in the Reichsarbeitsdienst (RAD, or German Work Service, a civilian organization much like the American Civilian Conservation Corps) prior to compulsory military service. In 1939, this requirement was extended to women (who served in the female equivalent, the RAD/wJ). Uniforms were characterized by a very distinct hat and a patch with a white shovel on a black background, with unit designations in red on the left shoulder above the Nazi armband (*above*). These women all wear men's RAD uniforms, and apart from the woman on the right, they appear quite amused to do so. (approx. $2\frac{1}{4}$" x $3\frac{1}{2}$" each)

## In Pairs and in Groups

We have all heard the adage "there's safety in numbers." Interestingly enough, there is research regarding pairs of people when it comes to leadership and group identity.

Derek Sivers refers to this as the first-follower principle. He states that "it takes an individual to be a leader; someone has to be first." If, as Sivers points out, no one follows that first person, he or she is nothing more than a loner. This can be hazardous if one happens to be the first primate to come down from the trees or the first soldier over the top into No Man's Land; if no one follows, one is not a leader so much as a target. However, the first person to *follow* that loner is every bit a leader as the one who set off in the first place; this second person validates the action of the first to the rest of the group. Since groups observe prior to acting—to see whether the leader has a good idea or is just stupid—once someone else joins the loner, it is no longer about him; it is about them. The primary follower leads others to follow.

Two or more people doing something strange or different is not always about peer pressure, even when that could be a factor. Photographs of pairs of women in their husbands' uniforms could well fit Sivers's first-follower model, and not just, "I'll do it if you will." Three women wearing their husbands' uniforms, or even more, almost certainly are. There are instances where a lone woman wearing her husband's uniform appears to be uncomfortable having her picture taken. Two or more women, almost without exception, all tend to be laughing and enjoying themselves. Once again, there is safety in numbers. If one woman feels awkward cross-dressing by herself, two, three, or even more validate her action, so the embarrassment is reduced and everyone can laugh about it together. No one is singled out for what might otherwise be considered aberrant or deviant behavior; instead, the focus is on a good laugh.

Figure 3-228. Wearing early war Heer *feldmützen* (field caps), these women pose for their photographer, the shadow of whose head can be seen in the foreground.

Figure 3-229. An exceptionally rare photograph of two women wearing men's overcoats of Organization Todt (OT), a civilian engineering and construction organization formed by Dr. Fritz Todt. Once the war started, OT was also responsible for a number of military engineering projects, such as the Atlantic Wall and V-1 and V-2 sites in France.

Figure 3-230. The photographer of these women wearing Heer *feldblusen* and *schiffchen* was apparently jostled as he took the picture. The three women have either been distracted or are posing for a second photographer to the left.

Figure 3-231. This photo was taken late in the war (the einheitsfeldmütze was not issued until 1943), of two women who wear Heer uniforms–one of a decorated *unteroffizier* with the Ostfrontmedaille ribbon in the second buttonhole, the other of an inexperienced *oberschützer*.

Figure 3-232. Probably taken prior to the war, these three women wear *schirmmützen* with a *waffenrock* and model 1936–style *feldbluse* over their dresses.

Figure 3-233. These four women line up for an impromptu formation, commanded by the *gefreiter* at the right. All four wear the *marschstiefel*–quite the comical sight when worn beneath dresses and skirts.

Figure 3-234. A *landser* poses with two women in M-36 *feldblusen*, one of which belongs to a *gefreiter*. Note that the collar *litzen*–the double striped insignia of the Heer–have not yet been sewn onto the uniforms.

Figure 3-235. These women wear the *schiffchen* and *schirmmütze* of a Luftwaffe friend. The glare from the leather chinstrap of the *schirmmütze* almost looks like the metallic strap of an officer.

Figure 3-236. These two women have joined each other outdoors; one wears a *gefreiter*'s dress uniform, while the other has added only the *feldmütze* to her repertoire.

Figure 3-237. Looking as if they were standing guard at an emplacement, these three women wearing *stahlhelm* and *mantel* and carrying Mauser K98k rifles pose beside a bin of some sort. A similarly constructed building is visible in the background.

Figure 3-238. These four *soldaten* have handed their *schiffchen* off to their female compatriots.

Figure 3-239. A rather jovial family portrait of *soldaten* and ladies leads one to wonder whether alcoholic beverages might have been involved. Some of the *soldaten* wear drillichanzuge (fatigue uniforms normally reserved for work details), one of whom flirts with a teddy bear. (3" x 4 5/8")

Figure 3-240. Four women salute from the exterior of a building with Bavarian-style shutters, perhaps on a *gebirgsjägerkaserne* (mountain troop base). Each of them wears einheitsfeldmütze and early-war overcoat.

Fifgure 3-242. These women in *unteroffizier* uniforms stand watch over their front stoop. Both grasp the hilt of their bayonets, but a *portepee* dangles from that of the woman on the left, signifying a position of authority. (3 3/8" x 4 3/4")

Figure 3-241 (*right*). A mother-daughter pair in matching shoes and outfits pose in an interesting photo; the two of them wear a Heer *schiffchen*, *koppel* (belt), and *pistolentasche* (holster) for the P-08 Luger, as opposed to a uniform jacket or coat. (2 5/8" x 3 5/8")

Figures 3-243 and 3-244. A woman identified as Else poses with her compatriots, one wearing a 1940 Heer uniform, and one wearing a uniform of the previous war. In figure 3-268 Else makes "a sharp report."

Figures 3-245 and 3-246. Three women pose for a photographer, then for a second cameraman, while wearing *schiffchen* and *schirmmützen* in these pictures dated January 18, 1941. (2⁵/₈" x 3⁵/₈" each)

Figure 3-247. Two women pose by the side of a lake, wearing *feldblusen* and *schiffchen* over their dresses. Note how long the sleeves are on the woman on the left!

Figure 3-248. These three women each wear early-war Heer *feldmützen* and *feldblusen* over their dresses in what appears to be their backyard.

Figure 3-249. How these three women found themselves on a rural road posing for a photograph must have been an interesting tale. Each woman wears a model 1936 *feldbluse* and *feldmütze*, and mockingly puffs on a cigarette. On the basis of the lengths of their skirts, it's quite likely that this picture was taken prior to the war, in the mid-1930s. ($2^5/_8$" x $3^7/_8$")

Figure 3-250. Two women pose in their neighborhood: one wears a *feldbluse* and *schirmmütze*, while the other wears a *panzerbluse* (tank crewman jacket) and *schiffchen*. Since tank crews were issued both, it is quite possible that these uniforms belong to the same *soldat*.

Figure 3-251. Two women make a scene of *feldwebel* versus *landser*, as the busty woman on the right (who can't completely close her tunic) dresses down her *kamerad* on the left. Both wear *waffenrock* and *schirmmütze*. (2¹/₂" x 3¹/₂")

Figure 3-252. An eclectic gathering of uniforms and individuals: two senior NCOs entertain four women who have donned uniforms and pose with a child. They are all wearing Heer uniforms, though the woman on the lower right wears a *waffenrock* with a police *schirmmütze*. (2¹/₂" x 3⁵/₈")

Figure 3-253. This *soldat* sits between a brace of charming women, each of whom wear *schirmmützen*. He does not look old enough to be a combat veteran, but the badges on his uniform are the Imperial Verwundetenabzeichen in Schwarz (Wound Badge in Black) and at least one other Imperial badge (note the crown atop the badge in the center of the pocket).

Figure 3-254. Two women pose outdoors against a stucco wall in Kleinostheim, in Upper Bavaria near Frankfurt; one wears a *waffenrock* and *schirmmütze* and the other wears a *feldmütze* and *feldbluse* without the collar *litzen* or the Heeresadler (Army Eagle). German soldiers were required to sew their own insignia on their uniforms. It is quite likely this *soldat* simply hadn't gotten that far.

Figure 3-256. One woman wears a *gefreiter's* *feldbluse* and *einheitsfeldmütze*, while the other wears a Kriegsmarine *matrosengefreiter* yeoman's uniform, quite possibly her own.

Figure 3-255 (*below*). Two women pose for a second photographer. One wears a *mantel* and *schirmmütze*, while the other wears a Heer *schiffchen* with a white jacket of some sort, possibly a *drillich* or fatigue uniform. The reverse of the image has the inscription "*Feldwebel* (sergeant) Löhning and Frau Admiral(?)." ($2^5/_8$" x $3^3/_4$")

Figure 3-257. Two women pose together, one wearing a Kriegsmarine *oberbootsmann*'s (senior boatswain's) *überzieher* and *schirmmütze*.

Figure 3-258 (*above*). Two women pose in Kriegsmarine uniforms. The woman standing wears the uniform of a *oberbootsmannsmaat* (senior boatswain's mate) and *schiffchen*. The seated woman wears a *stabsoberbootsmann's* (staff senior boatswain's) uniform and *schirmmütze*. The ribbon in the button hole is the 1914 Iron Cross Second Class.

Figure 3-259. These three women wearing Kriegsmarine summer uniforms have gone a step further to improve their depiction of men, adding penciled-in mustaches and goatees.

Figures 3-260 and 3-261. In these rare photographs of women wearing both military and civilian men's clothing, one woman wears a Luftwaffe *feldwebel's* white *schirmmütze* and *tuchrock* with a first-model Luftwaffe dagger with *portepee*. (lower image reduced)

Figure 3-262. These two women wear the Luftwaffe *tuchrock*, *schirmmütze*, and belt and bayonet. They both have the *portepee* attached, signifying a position of authority, even though both uniforms only have the rank of *flieger*, the equivalent of a basic airman or private. (2⁷/₈" x 3¹/₄")

Figures 3-263 through 3-265. Three women wear Luftwaffe *manteln* and *schiffchen* while posing with their comrades—probably fellow nurses—at the miners' hospital at Langendreer, between Essen and Dortmund. ($2^7/_8$" x $3^7/_8$" each)

Figure 3-266. These two women salute from across the dinner table, both wearing a Luftwaffe *mantel* and *schiffchen*.

Figure 3-267. These two women pose beside a stucco wall, one dressed in a *gefreiter*'s *tuchrock*, while the other wears an *unteroffizier*'s *fliegerbluse* and *schirmmütze*. The poor quality of the photo makes identifying the badges on the *tuchrock* impossible.

Figures 3-268. In this photo from 1941, three women wear three different uniforms of a Luftwaffe *gefreiter*: the *fliegerbluse*, *tuchrock*, and *mantel*, with *schiffchen*en and shirmmütze.

Figure 3-269. Two women in Luftwaffe uniforms, one as a gefrieter and the other as an *unteroffizier*, stand at attention on the front step of what is presumably their home. As can be seen in figures 3-315 and 3-316, they are unaware that an interestingly attired comrade is about to join them.

Figure 3-270. Four women, three of whom wear Luftwaffe *schirmmützen*, primp and prepare for a picture, though only one of them seems aware that the photographer has already started.

Figure 3-271. Three women wearing Luftwaffe *fliegerblusen* and *schiffchenen* salute a fourth who wears a *fliegerbluse* with the double tresse of a *Hauptfeldwebel* or "Spiess" on the cuff.

Figure 3-272. These two women both wear the *fliegerbluse* and *schiffchen* of a Luftwaffe *unteroffizier*, each of whom have been awarded the Iron Cross Second Class. Except for their shoes, which are hardly regulation, the cuff insignia of a flak crewman and their tired appearance might lead one to believe they are wearing their own uniforms, and not someone else's.

Figure 3-273 (*right*). Again, two women who wear uniforms of different services. The Luftwaffe uniform on the left has characteristic white *kragenspiegel* and cuffband of the Hermann Göring Division. (2 1/2" x 3 1/2")

Figures 3-274. Two women pose in Luftwaffe *obergefreiters' fliegerblusen* and *schiffchen*, one of which has what appears to be ribbons for la Cruz Blanca del Merito Militar de 1e Clase (Spanish White Cross of Military Merit) and Spanischen Freiheitskampf Feldzugsmedaille (Spanish Campaign Medal), which was not unusual for Luftwaffe members of the Condor Legion who fought in the Spanish Civil War. (2 7/8" x 4 1/4")

Figure 3-275. These women wear the *mantel*, *feldmütze*, and *marschstiefel* of their respective *männer*, one of whom served in the Heer and the other the Luftwaffe.

Figures 3-276 and 3-277. Two photographs of a man in a Luftwaffe *fliegerbluse* and two female companions, one of whom wears the insignia of a *regierungsassessor*, or government official (often a lawyer). It is possible the uniform is her own, but there were few female lawyers in the Third Reich.

Figure 3-278. A family celebrates their returning RAD members in Pfingsten in 1937. Everyone is wearing various pieces of RAD uniforms, with the exception of the man at the far left in a Heer *waffenrock* and the woman in the center, who wears his *schimmütze*.

Figure 3-279. These two women each wear a *schiffchen* with RAD insignia, as well as a *regenmantel* (raincoat, which was more of a rain cape). Buttoned slits to either side allowed one to reach through from under the cape, as both women grasp the handle of a large shovel or pick.

Figures 3-280 through 3-284. Like the women in figure 2-28, these women work in a uniform facility, in this case making hats for the Wehrmacht. They took a moment from their busy schedule to have a little fun with their products, posing with *feldmützen* and half-completed *schirmmützen*.

# A Fair Trade

While female-to-male cross-dressing in Western culture can be understood as an attempt to transcend a woman's subservient role, male-to-female cross-dressing, especially in the Third Reich, is more complex.

To this day, the cross-dressing antics of Bugs Bunny and plays and films such as *Some Like It Hot* (1959), *La Cage aux Folles* (1973/1978), and *To Wong Foo, with Love, Julie Newmar* (1995) elicit laughter. Call it what one will, eonism, transvestism, or cross-dressing is hardly a modern phenomenon, particularly when employed for comedic effect. Men, particularly adolescent men, have dressed as and portrayed women across stages in Europe as far back as Homer, and in China even earlier.

The term "transvestism" was first defined by Dr. Magnus Hirschfeld in 1910 as "the impulse to assume the external garb of a sex which is apparently not that of the subject as indicated by the sexual organs." For an established physician to have written about this behavior in the first decade of the twentieth century, particularly noting that transvestism is definitively *not* homosexuality, is indicative that cross-dressing not associated with the theater had been around for quite some time. In fact, if one examines the number of photographs of "bearded women" and circus sideshows of the late nineteenth century, few of them could be considered the least bit feminine (apart from their clothing), and one genuinely wonders whether they were women at all.

Figure 3-285. The "phenomenon" of the bearded woman could well be examples of early transvestism. This photo postcard from 1875 of Madame Proudhon of Bourth in Normandy is certainly enough to make one wonder. (3⅝" x 5½")

Transvestism and homosexuality were not unheard of in Europe, particularly in Germany; Berlin was especially well-known for its gay culture and cabarets during the 1920s and very early '30s. (In fact, the gay rights movement can trace its origin to Germany and Karl Heinrich Ulrichs as far back as the 1860s.)

Figure 3-286. This prewar photo proves that one did not have to wait for war to break out for the cross-dressing trend to begin. Here, men of the Sturmabteilung (SA) and women pose for the camera wearing their (or rather, each other's) best clothes.

This is not to say that promiscuity in Germany following World War I was exclusively homosexual. The Roaring Twenties in the Weimar Republic abounded with excesses, most of which were sexual. Just as medieval Europeans had done following the Black Death of the fourteenth century, Germans reveled in amazement that they had survived the Great War, questioning fate and their existence and throwing modesty to the four winds. Gay culture remained covert, but everyone seemed to know about it. Germans may not have accepted homosexuality, but they certainly accepted that it existed

This changed drastically in 1934, following the Night of Long Knives and the murder of Ernst Röhm, leader of the Sturmabteilung (*SA*, Storm Troopers). The Nazis used Röhm's homosexuality as an excuse to purge the SA and court the Wehrmacht, who were threatened by the SA's membership of over 2.5 million. Heinrich Himmler, who assumed control of the SA in the name of the Führer, led the way for strict antigay laws and enforced them to the best of his ability, interning thousands of homosexuals in the new concentration camps alongside political dissidents and offensive intelligentsia long before Jews became targeted internees.

Not every German man who put on a dress was a transvestite or gay, and if they were, they certainly did not admit it, especially given Himmler's zeal at incarceration, but images do exist of *soldaten* and their wives in which both traded clothing instead of just the woman. For the most part, this was undertaken in the spirit of the fun and silliness that was intended, though some men are far from pleased with the arrangement, as evidenced by their expressions. Transvestism was considered a sexual perversion both by psychiatrists and the Party, and to have photographic proof of the "transgression" was something with which some men were decidedly uncomfortable. Still, the majority of photographs of men wearing their wives' clothing as their women wore theirs captured sincerely humorous moments. How many beers or schnapps might have been involved before clothing was traded, or whether any were involved at all, remains unknown. The whole affair was frequently done for comedic effect, as if the individuals in the photos considered themselves within a modern-day equivalent of *As You Like It* or *The Twelfth Night.*

Most of the men in these photos wear only their wives' coats, primarily because it appears that little else would fit them. On the other hand, some go so far as to don dress, coat, hat, purse, and even shoes (though the truly hilarious images are of those men who wear everything but their wives' shoes, opting instead to wear their *marschstiefel* [marching boots or jack boots] with the wife's dress). The men seem determined to complete the ensemble, just as their wives have chosen to wear the entire uniform, belt, hat, or even more. When greater discrepancies in size occur, they are most immediately apparent in sleeve length. *Soldaten*'s gibbon-like arms protruding beneath the stylish short cuffs of a ladies' coat or dress make some of these images all the more ridiculous.

Figure 3-287. Visiting *soldaten* of the Panzerjäger Abteilung of Infanterie Regiment 97 and women trade hats in Bad Nenndorf, a small town outside Hanover. The *soldat* on the right is particularly amusing, wearing a kerchief and fur hat. (slightly enlarged.)

Figures 3-288 and 3-289. The photo at left is an example of the playful nature of group photos in which men and women trade clothing. Note the gentlemen wearing both men's and women's civilian hats, fur stoles, ladies' gloves, and even a cotton ball mustache and pie tin hat. In figure 3-289 (*below*), the *soldat* is the one in the middle wearing the woman's hat; the one in uniform is his wife.

Figures 3-290 through 3-292. This series of photographs, in which everyone appears to be wearing everyone else's clothing, male or female, leads one to wonder what beverages may have been involved. The sign "reserves at rest" could just as easily be translated to read "reserves at play," given the nature of the pictures. (3" x 3⁷/₈" each)

Figure 3-293. In this complete switch, the *soldat*'s wife wears his boots, uniform, and hat, while he wears her shoes, dress, and hat, though he wears his service shirt underneath. If one looks closely, his dark sport shorts can be seen beneath the weave of the dress.

Figure 3-294. It is difficult to determine who is more amused by this couple's switch in this picture taken on November 10, 1939, in Rodenbach. The *soldat* appears to be struggling to keep a straight face.

Figure 3-295. Reminiscent of figures 3-3 through 3-7, these men and their wives adjust one another's apparel in preparation for the "official" photograph, apparently unaware that an "unofficial" picture is being snapped.

Figures 3-296 and 3-297. The same couple, photographed in two different seasons, appear to have grown more accustomed to the idea of switching clothing; the mood in the second photo is considerably more lighthearted than the first. Note that the ladies' hat is the same in each.

Figure 3-298. This *soldat* (*right*) pinches the cheek of her presumably misbehaving counterpart, who wears her dress, apron, coat, hat, shoes, and even stockings.

Figures 3-299 and 3-300. Looking more like a band of wayward gypsies than *soldaten*, these men surround a *soldatin* to serenade and otherwise woo her with accordions and a mandolin. In figure 3-300 the ruse has apparently worked, and she joins them on a harmonica. ($2^5/_8$" x $3^3/_4$")

Figure 3-301. This lucky *soldat* relaxes arm in arm with two ladies, he wearing a checked blouse and apron, while the women wear his tunics, each bearing an artillerist's specialist badge on the left cuff and black wound badge on the pocket.

Figure 3-302. These three couples (note the pair cut off at the top of the image) have traded only their hats for this picture. The *soldat* on the right appears personally honored to be wearing his lady's hat.

Figures 3-303 and 3-304. This *soldat* has quite the sense of humor as the only male to wear hat, dress, and open-toed shoes as he poses in these two photos with the women wearing uniforms.

Figure 3-305. In this uncommon mid- to late-war photo, note the *feldhosen* (field trousers), *schnürrstiefel*, and *gemaschen* (short boots and gaiters) the *soldat* is wearing; both are obviously amused wearing each other's clothing.

Figure 3-306. Another later-war photo (*left*) shows a woman wearing her husband's *einheitsfeldmütze* and *panzerjacke* (tankers' jacket) with Panzer Assault Badge and expert mechanic's specialist badge on the cuff, while the *gefreiter* wears his wife's coat, gloves, and what appears to be floral wedding cap.

Figure 3-307. This *matrose* (sailor) wears his girlfriend's dress, pearls, and gloves, while she wears his *tellermütze*, presumably aboard the pocket battleship *Admiral Graf Spee*, as denoted by the tally on his cap. ($1^7/_8$" x $2^1/_2$")

Figure 3-308. Three uniformed women (one as a Heer *soldat* and two as Kriegsmarine *matrosen*) surround this man dressed in a ladies' nurse's uniform. His hair has been "pulled" into a hair net, probably just pinned to the hair at the back of his head, and he has even donned lipstick to complete his impression. ($3^{1}/_{8}$" x $4^{1}/_{2}$")

Figure 3-309. While she wears his Luftwaffe uniform, one gentleman behind her wears what appears to be her blouse and a flowered apron, while the other wears her hat. This picture also answers the question whether alcoholic beverages might at times be involved.

Figure 3-310. The sailor from figure 3-144 enjoys a quiet evening at home with his pipe and girlfriend in his *tellermütze* and uniform, while he wears her hat. The notation on the back of the photo notes the picture was taken in 1941. On the wall above them is his photo in uniform, as well as that of his brother, over her head, in Heer uniform.

Figure 3-311. Flanked by two women in Luftwaffe *fliegerblusen*, this man happily sports his wife's coat and hat. Airman Drell and his wife posed with an unnamed friend in Schlesien on June 8, 1941, according to the writing on the back of the picture.

Figures 3-312 through 3-314. These three photographs were taken during the same outing; two Luftwaffe men and three women (the third, her hand visible in figure 3-312, probably took the other two). The women obviously consider their hats and coats on the two men much more humorous than them. (2½" x 3½" each)

Figures 3-315 and 3-316. These two photos show a man clad in a woman's dress, stylish apron, and turban-style hat with bow and his Luftwaffe companions from figure 3-269. He seems in good spirits in the first picture, though by the second, facing the ridicule of his fellow airmen, he is not as enthusiastic about his choice of apparel.

Figure 3-317. This picture (*below*) proves that not all men were averse to wearing their wives' or girlfriends' clothing in exchange for their own. This lively group of Luftwaffe flak crewmen (note the flak emblem on the cuff of the woman on the right) has traded jackets and hats with their respective female accomplices.

Figure 3-318. This woman, complete with full Luftwaffe uniform and penciled mustache and goatee, stands beside her husband or boyfriend, who wears her dress, as well as eye shadow and lipstick, though he has retained his Wehrmacht-issued socks with three rings at the top to indicate the size.

Figure 3-319. This couple has traded hats and winter coats. He wears her bandeau ear warmer and floral overcoat, while she wears his Luftwaffe coat and carries his *schirmmütze*, no doubt because the military cap stands no chance of fitting over her hair without messing it.

Figure 3-320. We are presuming the woman who wears this *soldat's* uniform is taking the above picture, or else this particular *soldat* is probably far more enthusiastic about wearing his wife's clothing than he should be. His *kameraden* do not appear to be too worried.

Figure 3-321. The man in this photo has donned the woman's outfit, but in this case, it is her uniform that he wears. The cuff band and lightning bolt emblem on both her *feldmütze* and sleeve identify her as a member of the Nh (Nachrichtenhelferin) des Heeres, the female signals branch of the army.

Figure 4-1. The Fräulein Feldgrau theme so popular during the Great War was not limited to the depiction of young women; children were also depicted wearing uniforms, though the uniform was often their size and not that of their father's. This postcard was sent in 1915 to Miss Läse Günther-Harbung and her parents from Training Battalion 4 of Infantry Regiment 74.

# 4

# Die Kinder

Children naturally emulate and idolize their parents; it is a vital part of the learning process in which children are enculturated and prepared to assume their role in society. They copy adults by engaging in what psychologists call overimitation, which is unique to humans. Juvenile primates copy adult primates, but only if they deem an action to be relevant or necessary to achieve a desired result. If they consider an action irrelevant to what they want, they simply will not copy it, whereas human children will.

Part of this process involves dress-up play. Children see the clothes and uniforms adults wear every day, so they imitate their parents by trying on the same clothes. Psychologically, this establishes many of the gender identities and roles they will develop, but also reinforces the fact that they are not yet ready to take their place in society and have some growing to do, given that the clothes often fit them like tents, as the following pages illustrate.

It is not surprising to find that adolescents today identify with the prestige of brand name clothing. Marie J. Lachance, Pierre Beaudoin, and Jean Robitaille have researched the importance of brand as a socializing agent for boys and girls and have determined that "for both genders, brand sensitivity is related to peer influence" and "peers represent the most important predictor" (Lachance 2003, p. 47). Children are especially susceptible to peer pressure; they thrive on acceptance and sink into despondence or depression when spurned.

The children of the Third Reich were no different. Peer approval represents an important predictor in social development, and the Nazi Party was acutely aware of it. The Party included and openly recruited children. The Nazis welcomed one and all, regardless of social strata or economic status. Once the war started, even nationality held little influence over acceptance. If a young boy or girl could not find acceptance in a clique in the schoolyard or at home, there was always *one* clique that would include them; the youth of today would be the Party faithful of tomorrow.

Figure 4-2. Another diminutive comrade of fräulein feldgrau, this young girl sits enjoying her pipe and reading the latest war news, "We have once again done well!" By the time this card was written (June 28, 1918) news from the front was anything but, for although the Reichsheer was fighting bravely, they were being continually forced back by the Allies. ($3\frac{5}{8}$" x $5\frac{1}{2}$")

Young boys naturally emulate their fathers. At an early age they identify with patriarchal dominance in the family and develop sexual and gender identity, as well as masculine character, all by observing the father-mother relationship (this varies wildly across cultures but was especially true for Western culture during the early twentieth century). Even if the mother ruled the home and raised the children, young boys accepted their mothers' direction but still associated themselves with their fathers.

On the other hand, Lachance, Beaudoin, and Robitaille point out that young girls' modern brand sensitivity is "related to the importance *fathers* give to clothing brands [emphasis mine]," not mothers (ibid). Like boys, girls look to the father-mother relationship to develop sexual and gender identity, but according to Henry Biller and Stephan Weiss's interpretation of Helene Deutsch, fathers play an important function in leading girls' "erotic passive mode of interacting with males" (Biller, Weiss 1970, p. 79). A father who shows little attention to his daughter can be quite injurious, especially in her ability to form lasting relationships. In the case of this form of commercial recognition, a girl places importance on which clothing brands her father prefers; if she selects that brand, it becomes a de facto acceptance of her.

Brand approval and identification are akin to tribalism and admission into the tribe, something that was once a matter of life or death for early hominids and that still drives certain aspects of social behavior to this day. In a way, this is much like sports fandom; people wear the regalia of a football team or hockey club to identify themselves as part of that "tribe," but more importantly, to identify each other. Brands work in much the same way, acting as the regalia of that tribe.

Brand was every bit as important during the 1930s as it is today, perhaps even more so. Instead of being drawn to the Gap or Old Navy, the brand that children of Germany were drawn to was that of the Nazi Party. This was not by mistake; the Party placed its emblem on everything, from stamps, radios, and books, to schools, to public and private buildings, and at sponsored festivals. The Nazis created an identity that projected the affirmation that they provided services, welfare, and money, not just the state. As a result, *soldaten* fulfilled two major roles to their children: those of the father role model and masculine ideal, and of the immediate representative of the tribe (brand) leader. To wear a father's uniform was not only to emulate and be accepted by him, but to become a member of his, and that of the entire country's, brand.

This was a level of acceptance that transcended local peer groups, forming a nationwide brand bond that created a cultural cohesion that no other country in the world could match at that time. It certainly explains why Germany was as strong as it was, especially since the country comprised only 13 percent of Europe's population in 1930, and why it held out for as long as it did, until its utter destruction at the end of the war.

Figure 4-3. This young *schaffnerin* (female conductor) struggles to keep the cap of her Reichsbahn uniform from falling over her eyes (pre-1933). Complete with money changer and ticket satchel, she is almost ready to take her place alongside her female comrades shown in figures 2-36 through 2-38.

Figure 4-4 Two children play at a little-appreciated aspect of military life: being written up by one's superior. The child on the left has the cuff stripes of the *hauptfeldwebel*, or "Spiess." He is noting his friend's name in his book from the identification in his *schiffchen*. There are a number of images available to the collector of children wearing uniforms that were made for them, both Allied and Axis; the author encourages readers to look beyond the purview of this book to discover such fascinating photos!

Figure 4-5. Children join the excitement in their town as the Heer takes a break during a march (note the rows of gear placed behind them). The two children wear a helmet and 1938 *feldmütze*. The boy uses an upended gas mask canister as a seat to display his prowess on the drum.

Figure 4-6. These children are hard at their chores, clearing the stoop of snow. The girl in the background wears her father's *schiffchen* and boots, the latter of which are no doubt keeping her feet drier than her friend's shoes.

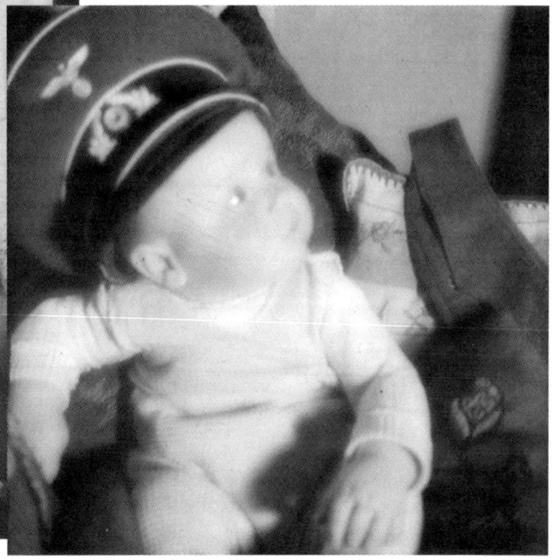

Figures 4-7 and 4-8. These were enlarged from their original negatives and show a baby who is not entirely sure about having his father's hat on his head. (each approximately $2^1/_4$" square)

Figure 4-9 (*right*). This young man from Thüringen wears his father's *feldmütze*.

Figure 4-10. This youngster wears his father's 1936 model service tunic; the dark-green collar and pleated pockets with scalloped flaps are typical of this issue. ($3^1/_8$" x $4^7/_8$")

Figure 4-11. This happy boy appears to be wearing his father's complete uniform of *schiffchen*, tunic, belt, bayonet, and boots. We don't know whether he also wears the trousers, since the tunic falls to the top of his boots, obscuring them.

Figure 4-12. This jovial young man wears his father's 1936 model uniform and 1938 model *schiffchen*. The insignia on the sleeve, just visible at the bottom of the photo, is that of an *oberschütze*, the equivalent of an private first class in the US Army or Marines.

Figure 4-13. It is not certain whether this *soldat* is a cavalryman or whether this is only the family farm horse, but this boy wears his father's *feldmütze* and his own Hitler Youth uniform. (3⁵/₈" x 5³/₈")

Figure 4-14. This girl wears her father's 1940 model *unteroffizier*'s uniform. Her father has earned the Infantry Assault Badge, probably in the Battle of France.

Figures 4-15 and 4-16. Two photos of the same girl from different prints, though probably taken the same day. She wears a *feldmütze*, an *unteroffizier*'s 1936 model uniform, and *marschstiefel*, though one can only see the tops of her boots in the smaller of the two pictures.

Figure 4-17. This boy wears the 1936 tunic of an *unteroffizier* (corporal), signified by the silver *tresse* (braid) on the collar and epaulets. The badges were issued prior to hostilities: what appears to be the 1931 SA Braunschweig badge on the left and the SA Sport Badge.

Figures 4-18 and 4-19. The boy (left) is ready to join his father in combat, wearing his 1943 model *einheitsfeldmütze* and tunic and carrying the K98 Mauser rifle. Note the simplified cut of the pockets and flaps. Meanwhile, the child on the right, dwarfed from within his father's 1936 *leutnant*'s tunic and boots, appears to be enjoying himself immensely. Although the uniform is an early pattern, father has already earned the Wound Badge in Black and an Iron Cross ribbon above the pocket.

Figure 4-20. These two young men, probably brothers, wear their father's *feldmütze* and helmet, as well as his service belt. While one youngster wears his own toy sword on an SA belt, the other wears his father's Heer belt and bayonet like a sword and baldric. (3 3/4" x 5 5/8")

Figure 4-21. This child seems to be prepared to face the worst the Allies can throw at him wearing father's 1940 model uniform, *feldmütze*, and gas mask.

Figure 4-22. This toddler is wearing his father's Heer *schirmmütze* (peaked cap) and has his trousers bloused in true military fashion.

Figure 4-23. Mother and son report to each other during Christmas / New Year of 1939/1940. This period between the invasion of Poland and the attack on the Low Countries is better known as the "Sitzkrieg" (Sitting War), when the Allies and the Axis did little more than stare at each other across the Siegfried and Maginot lines.

Figure 4-24. This toddler wears his father's *schirmmütze* as he enjoys a bright afternoon on the backyard bench.

Figures 4-25 and 4-26. This mother joins her son as he poses with his father's helmet and Mauser rifle. The reverse of the photo points out that the boy is "the youngest soldier on the tin roof." (Back of photo has been reduced.)

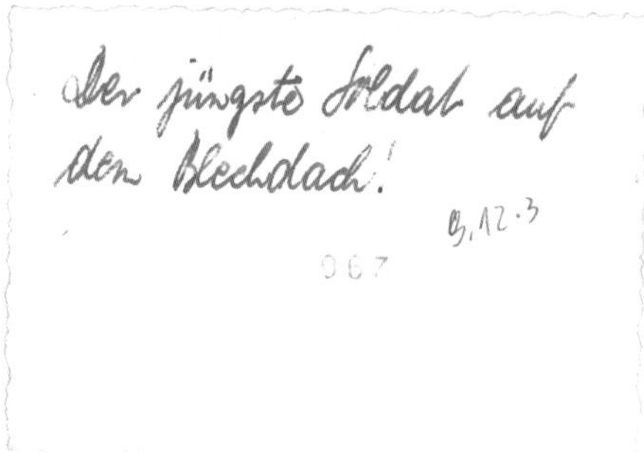

Figure 4-27. This young man seems to be more confused about his *schiffchen* and belt; his inquisitive father looks on from behind him.

Figure 4-28. These four young boys have come across a military convoy that has stopped somewhere near Frankenburg, Germany, in 1942. Three of them have borrowed helmets to pose for their hosts.

Figure 4-29. This young boy, wearing his own navy-style shirt, wears his father's officer *schirmmütze* and Heer dagger with *portepee*. ($2^7/_8$" x $3^1/_4$")

Figure 4-30. This girl, wearing her father's 1936 model *obergefreiter*'s (senior corporal) uniform bearing a Wound Badge in Black on the pocket, seems less than pleased to have to pose for this snapshot.

Figure 4-31. Wearing the 1936 model *unteroffizier*'s uniform, *feldmütze*, and boots, this lad seems quite pleased to look just like his father, clear down to the cigarette between his fingers.

Figure 4-32. Probably more pleased to see her father than to wear his *feldmütze*, this toddler exemplifies the bliss of innocence during wartime.

Figure 4-33. It's hard to say who is happier in this photo: young Peter Mumann wearing his father's Luftwaffe *schirmmütze* and belt with bayonet, or his younger sister Elisabeth. The back is noted "Kriegsjahr [war year] 1942." (approximately 2⁵/₈" square)

Figures 4-34 and 4-35. This boy wears his father's *feldmütze* and belt with bayonet. The reverse (reduced), which bears the date October 6, 1942, is inscribed "a friendly souvenir from your cousin Manfred."

Figure 4-36. This child's picture was taken while wearing a helmet during his visit to a 20-mm Flak gun during the Tag der Wehrmacht (Day of the Armed Forces) in 1940. Celebrated much like US Armed Forces Day, the Tag der Wehrmacht allowed civilians to visit displays hosted by the various branches of the military, in this case the Luftwaffe. Apart from bolstering the people's confidence in their armed forces, it also served as a powerful recruiting tool for the future manpower of the Reich.

Figure 4-37. Even with the cuffs of his father's *fliegerbluse* turned up, this Luftwaffe *flieger*'s son's fingers are barely visible. Although it is difficult to say for sure, the owner of this uniform was probably a Flak crewman; if the photo was in color, red collar insignia would verify this.

Figure 4-38. This young man seems perplexed to find himself in his father's *feldmütze* and *gefreiter*'s *fliegerbluse*. The reader, like the author, is no doubt equally perplexed as to why the child is in a basket.

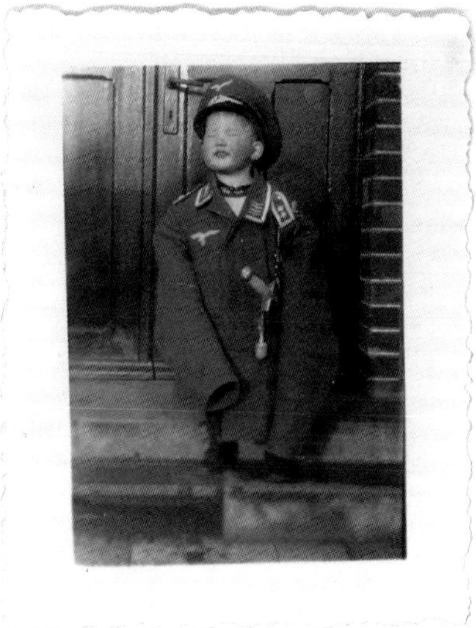

Figures 4-39 and 4-40. This jovial toddler seems to be both proud and amused; he wears his father's *fliegerbluse* like a tent. His father, a Luftwaffe *oberfedlwebel* (master sergeant), is certainly of a position of authority to merit the child's respect and admiration.

Figures 4-41 and 4-42. This boy wears his father's *unteroffizier*'s *fliegerbluse* and M-43 *einheitsfeldmütze* in the family's backyard. His sister, comfortable in father's lap, doesn't appear to be impressed.

Figure 4-43. This Luftwaffe *gefreiter*'s son stands guard over the family farm with his father's Mauser. This boy's father was definitely a Flak crewman; the badge on his chest is the Luftwaffe Flak Badge. ($3\frac{1}{2}$" x $5\frac{1}{4}$")

Figure 4-44. This boy wears his father's helmet and what appears to be his own rain cape while riding to save the Reich on his rocking horse.

Figure 4-45. Mother and daughter smile for the camera while wearing father's Kriegsmarine *tellermütze* (disk cap) and *schiffchen*. The boy, wearing (perhaps) his uncle's Heer *feldmütze*, grins alongside them. Everyone viewed military service in the Third Reich as an honor and responsibility; it was not unusual for entire families to serve in one post or another within the Wehrmacht. (enlarged 135%)

Figure 4-46. The woman in figure 3-144 sits with a youngster, probably her son, as he wears his father's Kriegsmarine uniform. The reverse states "a small souvenir of a cozy evening at Niftmanns" from March 1941.

Figure 4-47. Not all children modeled military uniforms; this young man appears to be quite happy to wear his father's cap from the Reichsarbeitsdients (National Labor Service, or RAD) while playing his drum in the family garden.

Figure 4-48. This young man stands at attention in his father's SS-Scharführer's (roughly equivalent to a US Army corporal) uniform and *schirmmütze*. Original photographs of SS personnel are rare compared to the other branches of the Wehrmacht; images of children wearing their father's SS uniform are considerably more so. (3¹/₈" x 4³/₈")

# Afterword

The tragedy of war touches so many lives, especially in a conflict as expansive and all-encompassing as World War II. Whole nations were involved, and even countries that saw no fighting on their shores faced adversities and difficulties exclusively their own. Even noncombatant nations had to deal with the conflict in one form or another.

The war impacted entire families on both sides, either by death or injury of loved ones or through interruptions and privations of daily life, such as separation, rationing, and other restrictions. Everyone sought ways to forget the war or to enjoy the happy moments when they could, and the soldiers of the Reich were no different. Like their Allied counterparts, the *soldaten* on leave wanted high-quality time with their families and friends, as well as a chance to relax and laugh a little.

Little identifies the owners of these uniforms—the husbands, boyfriends, and fathers who lent the accoutrements of war to their loved ones for each other's amusement—and their fates remain a mystery. Whether they made their way home, perished on the battlefield, or were left to starve and die in some frigid prisoner-of-war camp also raises the question of what happened to the women in these pictures. Many of these photos were lifted from deteriorating scrapbooks or were found loose in forgotten trunks and boxes in the many attics of Europe; their names and fates remain largely unknown. There was even a chance that some of the women and children in these photos perished as the Allies closed in on the Reich, either from bombing or simply by being in the wrong place at the wrong time as the front moved through their hometowns and cities. For the one brief moment when these pictures were taken, there was joviality at the uniforms that did not fit, and smiles at the absurdity of wearing them. The war was forgotten, the bombing did not matter, and families were together. Even if their lives were miserable or wracked with grief, for that instant at least they were happy.

# Appendix

# Appendix A
## Wehrmacht Insignia
### Collar, Shoulder, and Sleeve Insignia
### das Heer

| Rank | Collar Insignia | Shoulder Insignia | Sleeve Insignia |
|---|---|---|---|
| Schützer | | | |
| Oberschützer | | | |
| Gefreiter | | | |
| Obergefreiter | | | |
| Unteroffizier | | | |
| Unterfeldwebel | | | |
| Feldwebel | | | |
| Oberfeldwebel | | | |
| Stabsfeldwebel | | | |

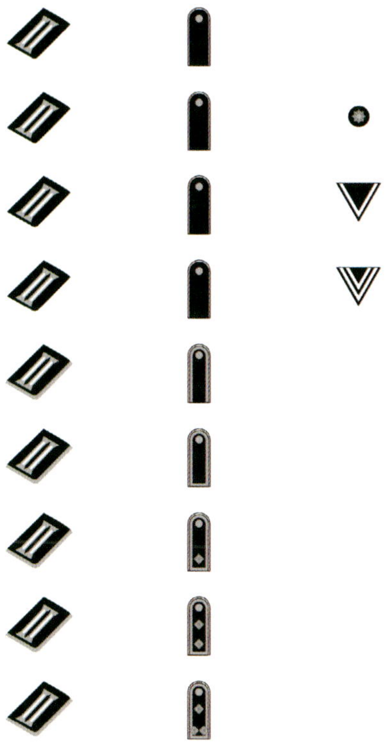

### Officer Insignia

| Rank | Collar Insignia | Shoulder Insignia |
|---|---|---|
| Leutnant | | |
| Oberleutnant | | |
| Hauptmann | | |

## Collar, Shoulder, and Sleeve Insignia

# die Luftwaffe

| Rank | Collar Insignia | Shoulder Insignia | Sleeve Insignia |
|---|---|---|---|
| Schützer | | | |
| Oberschützer | | | |
| Gefreiter | | | |
| Obergefreiter | | | |
| Unteroffizier | | | |
| Unterfeldwebel | | | |
| Feldwebel | | | |
| Oberfeldwebel | | | |
| Stabsfeldwebel | | | |

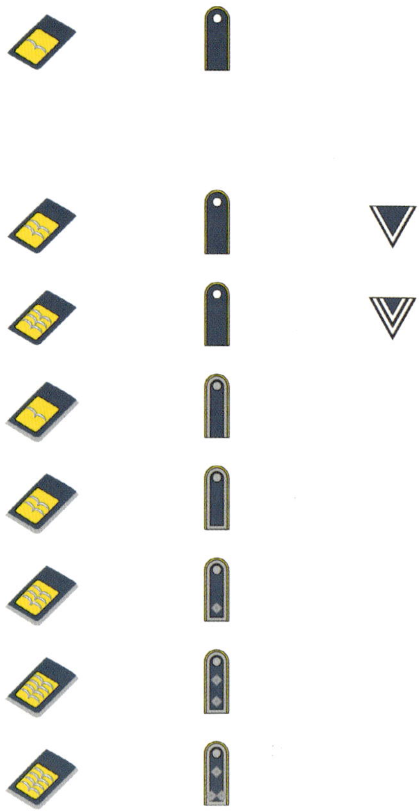

### Officer Insignia

| Rank | Collar Insignia | Shoulder Insignia |
|---|---|---|
| Leutnant | | |
| Oberleutnant | | |
| Hauptmann | | |

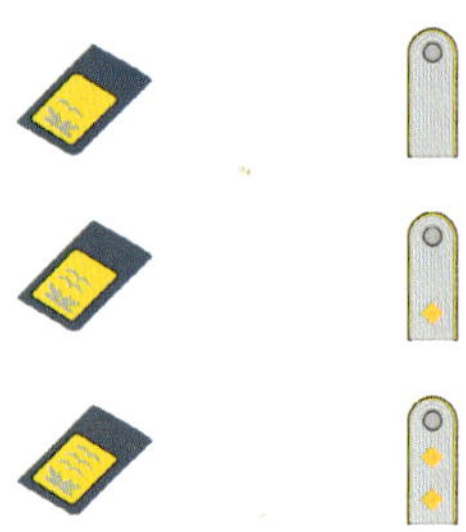

# Collar, Shoulder, and Sleeve Insignia

# die Kriegsmarine

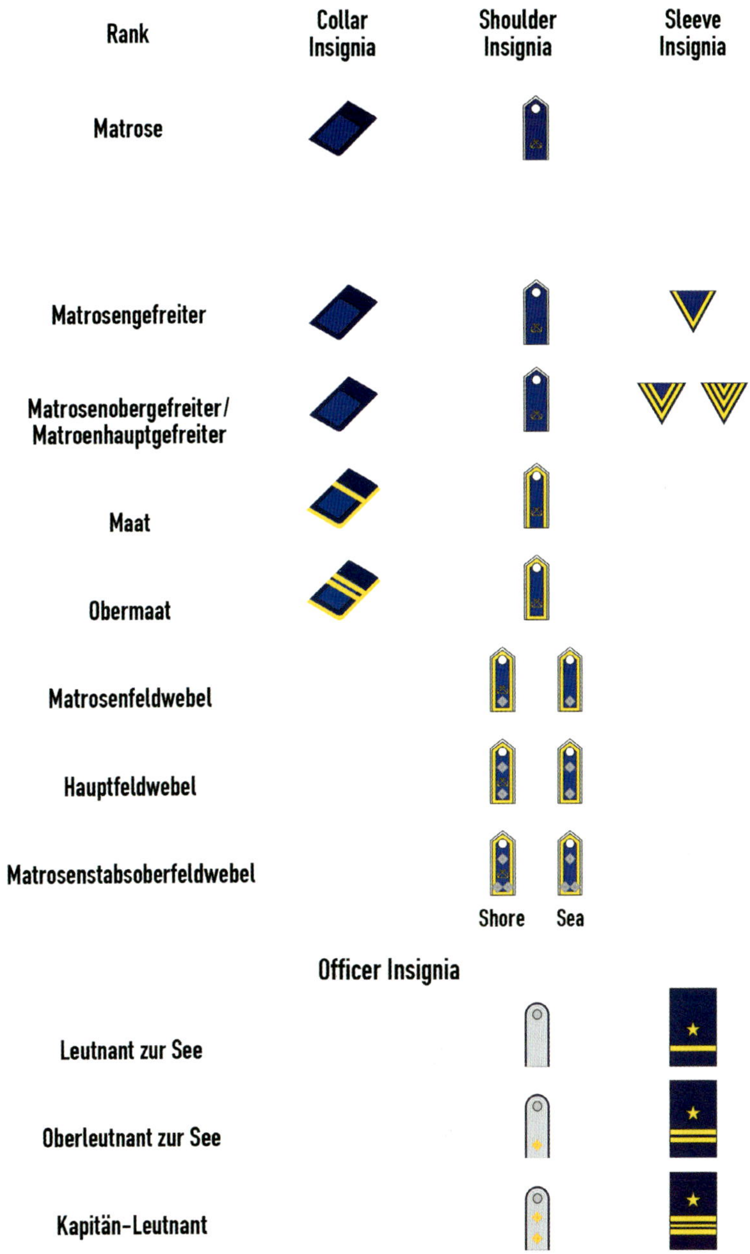

## Collar, Shoulder, and Sleeve Insignia
# die Waffen-SS

| Rank | Collar Insignia | Shoulder Insignia | Sleeve Insignia |
|---|---|---|---|
| SS-Schützer | | | |
| SS-Oberschützer | | | |
| SS-Sturmmann | | | |
| SS-Rottenführer | | | |
| SS-Unterscharführer | | | |
| SS-Scharführer | | | |
| SS-Oberscharführer | | | |
| SS-Hauptscharführer | | | |
| SS-Sturmscharführer | | | |

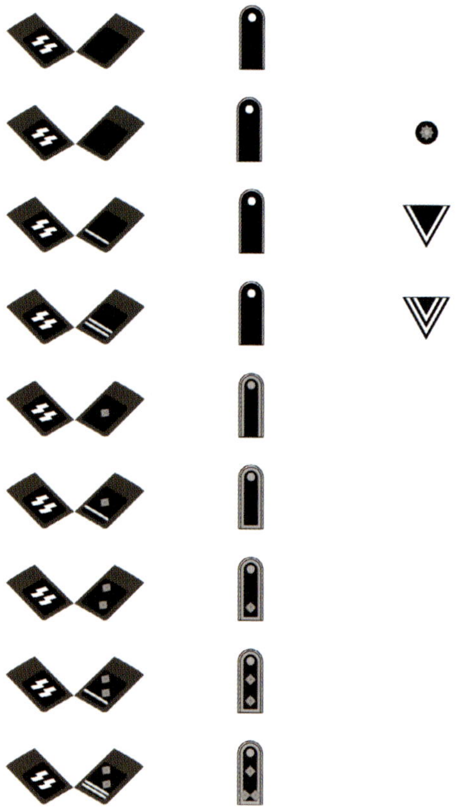

### Officer Insignia

| Rank | Collar Insignia | Shoulder Insignia | Sleeve Insignia |
|---|---|---|---|
| SS-Untersturmführer | | | |
| SS-Sturmführer | | | |
| SS-Hauptsturmführer | | | |

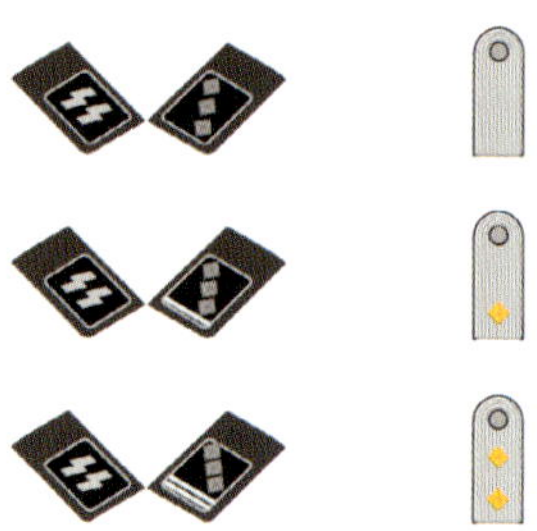

# Appendix B
## Glossary

*Afrika Korps* - German divisions that served in the North African campaign under Feld Marschall Erwin Rommel

*Agfa* - German camera and film company founded in 1867, now based in Belgium

*Aliierten* - The Allies

*Ansichtkarten* - Postcards

*Arbeitsmaiden* - Working maids or working women (youthfulness is implied)

*Bandenkampfabzeichen* - Anti-Partisan Badge

*Bermütze* - Mountain cap. A popular style of cap originally used by mountain troops and copied as the model 1943 *Einheitsfeldmütze*

*Brief* - Letter

*Brot* - Bread

*Calotype* - Early wet-plate photographic process using a plate made of paper instead of silver

*Cantinières* - Canteen staff of the Napoleonic French army; uniformed women who attended to the supply and victualing requirements of the soldiers and who also tended to the wounded on the battlefield

*Carte de visite* - Also known as a CDV by collectors

*Daguerreotype* - First successful commercial photographic process. The process was invented by Louis-Jacques-Mandé Daguerre in 1836 and relied on a silver plate coated with photoreactive chemicals

*Der Adler* – *The Eagle*; a Luftwaffe trade magazine

*Deutsche Arbeitsfront (DAF)* - German Labor Front. A uniformed civilian trade union organization of the Nazi Party

*Deutsches Rotes Kreuz* - German Red Cross

*Dienstauszeichen* - Service medal

*Dienstbrille* - Service glasses. Standardized glasses issued to German troops

*Dienstzeit* - Time of service

*Dirndl* - Traditional Bavarian and Austrian style of dress

*Donnerwetter Tadelos* - Literally "thunderweather flawless"; the phrase is comparable to uttering "darned fine" in English

*Drillichanzuge* - German fatigue uniform similar to that issued for field use, but often made of a white or ashen gray cotton

Dritten Reich – Third Reich

Ehrenkreuz des Weltkrieges 1914–1918 - Cross of Honor of the World War 1914–1918. Issued in 1934 to Great War veterans, the medal was also referred to as the Hindenburg Cross

*Errinerung* - Souvenir. Literally an item of memory

*Ersatz* - Substitute

Exacta - First single-lens reflex camera. The Exacta was made by Ihagee

Fallschirmschützenabzeichen - Paratrooper badge issued to German paratroopers upon completion of training

*Feldblau* - Field blue; a bluish-gray color used in Luftwaffe uniforms

*Feldbluse* - Field blouse. Standard German woolen field uniform shirt

*Feldgrau* - Field gray; a gray shade of green common to German field uniforms

*Feldkamera* - Field camera

*Feldmütze* - Field cap. Also referred to as a *schiffchen* (little ship) by German troops

*Feldwebel* - An NCO (noncommissioned officer) or sergeant

*Ferrotype* - Type of early photographic wet plate process. A metal plate coated with black enamel and coated with photoreactive chemicals. Also called "tintype."

*Flieger* - Pilot; also used to mean airman (Luftwaffe private)

*Fliegerabwehrkanone* (Flak) - Anti-aircraft cannon

*Fliegerbluse* - Flight tunic; standard service tunic for *Luftwaffe* personnel

*Fliegerhorst* - Air bases

*Flizstiefel* - German type of felt boots used on the Russian front

Flugmeldedienst - Air Reporting Service

*Flugzeug* - Airplane

Flugzeuggerät Tätigskeitabzeichen - Luftwaffe rating patch, literally the aircraft equipment occupation badge for mechanics

*Fraktur* - The heavy, characteristically German black letter typeface used since the sixteenth century

Franke & Heidecke - German camera company that invented the *Rolleicord* and Rolleiflex dual- or twin-lens reflex cameras

*Fräulein* - Miss; an unmarried woman

Fräulein Feldgrau - Miss Fieldgray, a popular pictorial theme of German postcards during the Great War featuring a woman in uniform

*Fronturlauber* - Vacationing soldier from the front

*Frühjahr* - Spring

*Frühling* - Spring

*Führer* - Leader. When used as *Der Führer*, it implied the leader of the Nazi Party, Adolf Hitler

*Gasthaus* - Guest house or inn

*Gefreiter* - An upper private/lower corporal; this was not a non-commissioned officer rank

*Gemaschen* - Gaiters, or a style of canvas ankle covering

*Gerät* – Apparatus

*Handschuen* - Gloves. Literally hand shoes

*Hauptfeldwebel* (*Spiess*) - Primary sergeant; an honorific title given to the senior sergeant of a unit. Also known as Spiess or "spear," the implement carried by seventeenth and eighteenth century noncommissioned officers as a symbol of their position

*Hauptmann* - Captain

*Haushalt* - Household

*das Heer* - The German Army

Hitlerjugend - The Hitler Youth

Hoheitszeichen - High Official Emblem. This is the displayed Nazi eagle and swastika

*Ihagee* - Industrie- und Handelsgesellschaft, or Industry and Trade Society. A German camera company based in Dresden (*Ihagee* is the German pronunciation for IHG)

*Kamera* - Camera

*Kamerad(-in)* - Comrade / female comrade. Adding *-in* to the end of a noun indicated that individual was female, like adding *-ess* to a noun in English

*Kaserne* - Military base or compound

*Kolberg* - Movie released in 1945 about the Napoleanic battle for the city of the same name. Created by the Nazi Propaganda Ministry and directed by Veit Harlan, the film is best known as one of the most wasteful films made at a time when the Third Reich could ill afford the material drain

*Korrespondenzkarte* - Correspondence card; archaic reference to a postcard

*Kradmantel* - Literally a cycling coat, a rubberized overcoat worn by military motorcyclists or those in inclement weather

*Kragenspiegel* - Rank or service insignia worn on the collars of German uniforms

*Krankenhaus* - Hospital

*Kreuzer* - Cruiser; a class of naval warship

*Kriegsberichter* - War reporter. German war reporters were not journalists, such as many American correspondents

*Kriegshilfsdienst* - War assistance service

*Kriegsjahr* - War year

Kupferstichschrift - Copper-plate script. Form of German handwriting practiced throughout the nineteenth and early twentieth centuries that mimicked a style of copperplate engraving. Common form of handwriting for soldiers during World War I.

*Kurrent* - Form of German handwriting practiced throughout the nineteenth and early twentieth centuries (see also *Kupferstichschrift*). Common form of handwriting for soldiers during World War I

*La fille du régiment* - *The Daughter of the Regiment*. An 1840 opera by Donizetti about a girl adopted by a military regiment. The theme was popular until the early twentieth century

*Landser* - Private in the German army. Interchangeable with the term *soldat* (soldier)

Leica - Camera invented by Oskar Barnack for Leitz that used a complicated multilens photographic lens that used a much-smaller 35 mm negative. Short for "Leitz Camera."

*Leicht* - Light

Leitz - German camera company founded by Ernst Leutz, originally an optics company making microscopes

*Leutnant* - Lieutenant

*die Luftwaffe* - The German air force, still referred to by this title today.

*Mannschaften* - Enlisted men (as opposed to officer ranks)

*Mantel* - Overcoat

*Marschstiefel* - Tall marching boots, better known as jack boots

*Matrose* - Sailor

*Merkblatt* - An informational leaflet

*Muster* - Pattern

*Nachrichtenhelferin* - Female signals/communications soldier

*Nationalsozialistische Flieger Korps* (*NSFK*) - National Socialist Flying Corps, an organization of the Nazi Party that trained pilots against the terms of the Treaty of Versailles

National-Sozialitische Deutsche Arbeiterpartei - National Socialist German Workers Party (Nazi Party)

*Oberbootsmann* - Senior boatswain

*Oberbootsmannsmaat* - Senior boatswain's mate

*Oberfähnrich* - Senior officer cadet

*Oberfeldwebel* - Senior sergeant; roughly equivalent to a US Army master sergeant

*Obergefreiter* - Senior lance corporal

Oberkommando der Luftwaffe - High Command of the *Luftwaffe*

Oberkommando der Wehrmacht - High Command of the *Wehrmacht*

*Oberschützer* - Senior private. This rank was usually conferred on an individual who showed promise as a leader but would not otherwise qualify as a *gefreiter*

*Ohne* - Without

Organization Todt (OT) - Uniformed civilian civil engineering and construction service organized by Dr. Fritz Todt

Ostfrontmedaille - Eastern Medal, the medal for service on the Russian front. Nicknamed the "frozen meat medal" by *soldaten*

*Panzergrenadier* - Soldier of the mechanized infantry

*Panzerjacke* - Tunic issued to German tank and tracked vehicle crews

*Panzerjäger* - Literally "tank hunter"; German antitank personnel

Panzerkampfabzeichen - Tank Battle Badge, issued to German tank crews after specified numbers of tank battles

*Patronenkiste* - Cartridge boxes worn on the belt. (plural form is *patronenkisten)*

*Pfeifenschnur* - Whistle lanyard

*Poileau* – French soldier

*Portepee* - Sword knot. When worn on a dagger or bayonet, this identified an elistedman in a position of authority

*Pullover* - Sweater

*Regenmantel* - Rain coat. Also rain cape

*Regierungspräsident* – The primary government office, particularly of a city

Reichsadler - Reich's Eagle, also referred to as the *hoheitszeichen*

*Reichsarbeitsdienst* - RAD, Reich Work Service or Force, similar to the American Civilian Conservation Corps

*Reichsbahn* - German State Railroad System

*Reichsheer* - Predecessor of the Wehrmacht; the German armed forces of Imperial Germany.

*Reichsmark* - The primary form of currency in Germany until 1948, when it was replaced by the Deutsch Mark (DM)

*Reichspfennig* - German Reich's penny. 100 reichspfennig = 1 reichsmark

Reichspost - German National Mail Service

Reichswehr - Army of Imperial Germany

Rolleicord - Twin-lens reflex camera manufactured by Franck & Heidecke

Rolleiflex - Twin-lens reflex camera also manufactured by Franck & Heidecke. The Rolleiflex line was a higher end camera that was popular into the 1970s.

*Säbel* - Saber

*Sanitäter* - Medic

*S-bahn* - Abbreviation for *strassenbahn*, or street railway system

*Schaffner(-in)* - Train official responsible for selling and validating passenger tickets

Schiessauszeichnung - Shooting award. This braided cord was worn from the right shoulder to the second closure button of the tunic

*Schiffchen* - "Little ship"; the nickname given by *soldaten* to the *feldmütze*

*Schirmmütze* - Peaked cap

*Schlips* - Necktie

*Schneiderei* - Tailoring shop

*Schnürstiefel* - Short, ankle-length boots

*Schulterklappen* - Rank insignia attached to the shoulder of Wehrmacht uniforms

*Schwer* - Heavy

*Segelflieger* - Glider pilot

*Soldat(-in)* - Soldier. Used as a title as well as a description

Sportabzeichen - Sports award. There were several in the Third Reich, but the most sought after was issued by the Sturmabteilung (SA)

*Stabsoberbootsmann* - Staff senior boatswain

*Stahlhelm* - Steel helmet

*Steuermannsmaat* - Coxswain's mate naval rating

Sturmabteilung (SA) - Assault Section, the military arm of the Nazi Party, better known today as the Brown Shirts for their uniform, or Storm Troopers

Sturmabzeichen - Assault Badge.

*Tellermütze* - Round sailor's hat

*Tintype - see Ferrotype*

*Tuchhosen* - Service trousers worn with the tuchrock and waffenrock dress uniform

*Tuchrock* - Service tunic

*U-bahn* - *Untergrundbahn*; underground railway or subway system

*Überzieher* - Naval peacoat, a heavy wool overcoat

*Unteroffizier* - Literally "under officer." Roughly equivalent to a corporal, the lowest noncommissioned officer rank of the Wehrmacht

*Vivandières* - Licensed businesswomen or wives / daughters of regimental victualers and non-military supply contractors in the nineteenth-century French army

*Vergeltungswaffen* – Vengeance weapons; this is what the "V" in V-1 and V-2 stood for

*Volksgasmaske* – People's gas mask

*Vorläufig* – Temporary or provisional

*Waffenfarbe* - Color designation for various specialties within each service

*Waffenrock* - Dress tunic of the Heer

Wehrmacht - The German armed forces of the Third Reich

*Wehrmachtangehörige* - Military personnel. Literally "Member of the Armed Forces."

Weimar Republik - The government of Germany during the interim between the imperial government of *Kaiser* Wilhelm II and the Third Reich

*Wochenschau* - Weekly newsreel report

*Wohnort* - Residence

Zeiss AG - German optics company that manufactured microscopes and cameras, among other industrial optics; founded by Carl Zeiss in 1846

Zeiss-Ikon - Primary camera line of Zeiss AG

*Zimmermansmaat* - Carpenter's mate naval rating.

# Bibliography


Allison, Nigel. *Collecting World War II German Military Pay & Service Books*. Shropshire, UK: Ulric of England, 2007.

Archambeau, Michael. "20 First Photos from the History of Photography." *PetaPixel.com*. May 21, 2015. petapixel.com/2015/05/23/20-first-photos-from-the-history-of-photography/.

Barlog, Friedrich. *Wir in der Heimat*. Berlin: Zeitgeschichte-Verlag, 1940.

Brandl, Dr. Ralph. *Blitz German*. Harrisburg, PA: Military Service Publishing, 1943.

Cardoza, Thomas. "Cantinières and Vivandières of the French Army." *Cantinieres.com*. 2010-2016. www.cantinieres.com.

——. "Myths and Falsehoods." *Cantinieres.com*. 2010-2016. www.cantinieres.com/myths.php.

Charman, Terry. *The German Home Front, 1939–45*. New York: Philosophical Library, 1989.

Cooph. " The History of Photography in 5 Minutes." *YouTube.com*. February 8, 2016. www.youtube.com/watch?v=JoxGEymA8ro.

Cowdery, Ray and Josephine Cowdery. *Papers Please!* Lakeville, MN: USM, 1996.

Cycleback , David Rudd. " Tintypes, Daguerreotypes and Ambrotypes." Photograph Identification Guide. *Cycleback.com*. 2003, 2005. www.cycleback.com/photoguide/dags.html.

Daniel, Malcolm. "Daguerre (1787–1851) and the Invention of Photography" Heilbrunn Timeline of Art History. Metropolitan Museum of Art. October 2004. www.metmuseum.org/toah/hd/dagu/hd_dagu.htm.

——. "The Daguerreian Age in France: 1839–1855." Heilbrunn Timeline of Art History. Metropolitan Museum of Art. October 2004. www.metmuseum.org/toah/hd/fdag/hd_fdag.htm.

——. "William Henry Fox Talbot (1800–1877) and the Invention of Photography." Heilbrunn Timeline of Art History. Metropolitan Museum of Art. October 2004. www.metmuseum.org/toah/hd/tlbt/hd_tlbt.htm.

Davis, Brian Leigh. *The German Home Front 1939–45*. Oxford: Osprey, 2007.

Edward. "Women in the Civil War: Vivandieres." The Gilder Lehrman Institute of American History. March 12, 2012. www.gilderlehrman.org/community/blog/women-civil-war-vivandieres.

Estabrooke, Edward M. *The Ferrotype and How to Make It*. 12th ed. New York and Chicago: Anthony and Scovill. 1903. Archive.org. archive.org/stream/ferrotypehowtoma00esta#page/n7/mode/2up.

Everett, Susanne. *Lost Berlin*. New York: Gallery Books, 1979.

Fineman, Mia. "Kodak and the Rise of Amateur Photography." Heilbrunn Timeline of Art History. Metropolitan Museum of Art. October 2004. www.metmuseum.org/toah/hd/kodk/hd_kodk.htm.

Friedrich, Otto. *Before the Deluge: A Portrait of Berlin in the 1920s*. New York: Fromm International. 1986.

Garson, Paul. *Album of the Damned: Snapshots From the Third Reich*. Chicago: Academy Chicago. 2008.

——. *New Images of Nazi Germany: A Photographic Collection*. Jefferson, NC: MacFarland. 2012.

Guenther, Irene. *Nazi Chic? Fashioning Women in the Third Reich*. Oxford and New York: Berg, 2004.

Guerin, Frances. *Through Amateur Eyes: Film and Photography in Nazi Germany*. Minneapolis: University of Minnesota Press, 2012.

Harding, Colin. "How to Spot a Collodion Positive, Also Known As An Ambrotype (early 1850s–1880s)." National Media Museum. April 24, 2013. blog.nationalmediamuseum.org.uk/find-out-when-a-photo-was-taken-identify-collodion-positive-ambrotype/.

——. "How to Spot a Carte De Visite (late 1850s–c. 1910)." National Media Museum. April 24, 2013. blog.nationalmediamuseum.org.uk/find-out-when-a-photo-was-taken-identify-a-carte-de-visite/.

Husband, Tony, Ed. *Cartoons of World War II*. London: Arcturus, 2015.

Klose, Dietrich. *Front und Heimat, Teil 2: Geschreibenes und Gedrucktes 1939–1945*. Karlsdorf, Germany: Historicmedia-Verlag, 2005.

Littlejohn, David. *Defending the Reich.* San Jose, CA: R. James Bender, 2007.

Mackenna, Sean. "History of the Wet Plate Colloidon [*sic*] Process." AlternativePhotography.com, n.d. www.alternativephotography.com/wp/history-colloidon-process/.

Mason, Chris. *Personal Effects of the German Soldier.* Atglen, PA: Schiffer, 2006.

McGregor, Malcolm. *The German Home Front, 1939–45.* Oxford: Osprey, 2007.

Osterman, Mark and France Scully Osterman. "What Is Collodion?" Scully & Osterman, n.d. www.collodion.org/q&a.html.

Rappaport, Helen. "No Place for Ladies: The Untold Story of Women in the Crimean War." NYU School of Medicine. April 17, 2010. medhum.med.nyu.edu/view/13132.

Roland, Paul. *Life in the Third Reich: Daily Life in Nazi Germany, 1933–1945.* London: Arcturus, 2016.

Sáiz, Augustín. *Deutsche Soldaten: Uniforms, Equipment & Personal Effects of the German Soldier, 1939–45.* Philadelphia and Newbury, UK: Casemate, 2008.

Samuel, Wolfgang. *German Boy: A Child in War.* New York: Broadway Books, 2001.

——. *The War of Our Childhood,* Jackson: University of Mississippi Press, 2002.

Tschöltsch, *Generalmajor E. Der Dienstunterricht in der Luftwaffe.* Berlin: E. S. Mittler & Sohn, 1942.

Wahren, Christopher. "19th Century Photographic Plate Sizes." Christopher Wahren Fine Photography, 2007-2008. cwfp.biz/platesizes.php.

Williamson, Gorden. *World War II German Women's Auxiliary Services.* Oxford: Osprey, 2003.

Wilson, Captain Barbara A., USAF (Ret.). "WWI: Thirty Thousand Women Were There." Military Women Veterans: Yesterday-Today-Tomorrow, 1996-2004. userpages.aug.com/captbarb/femvets4.html.

——. "Women in World War II." Military Women Veterans: Yesterday-Today-Tomorrow. 1996-2004. userpages.aug.com/captbarb/femvets4.html.

——. "An Outline History of Professional Photography in Sussex from 1841 to 1855." PhotoHistory-Sussex.co.uk, n.d. www.photohistory-sussex.co.uk/Sussexearly.htm.

——. "The Carte-de-Visite." Codex99.com, December 21, 2014. www.codex99.com/photography/49.html.

——. "The Daguerreotype Process." PhotoHistory-Sussex.co.uk, n.d. www.photohistory-sussex.co.uk/dagprocess.htm.

——. "Dating Ambrotype Photographs." PhotoTree.com, 2013. www.phototree.com/id_amb.htm.

——. *Duden Oxford Großwörterbuch Englisch*, Mannheim, Germany: Dudenverlag, 1990.

——. "Heritage." Kodak.com, 2016. www.kodak.com/ek/US/en/corp/aboutus/heritage/default.htm.

——. "History of Photography, 1826-1862." The Wizard of Photography. PBS.org, 1999-2000. www.pbs.org/wgbh/amex/eastman/timeline/index.html.

——. "Maisons Nicéphore Niépce." *Maisons des illustres. French Ministry of Culture.* n.d. www.photo-museum.org.

——. "Material Safety Data Sheet: Sodium Thiosulfate." Acros Organics, February 20, 2008. www.ch.ntu.edu.tw/~genchem99/msds/exp19/Na2S2O3.pdf.

——. "The Camera Obscura: Aristotle to Zahn." Adventures in Cybersound, April 20, 2008. web.archive.org/web/20080420165232/www.acmi.net.au/AIC/CAMERA_OBSCURA.html.

——. "Working with Photography Themes." Icon Photography School, 2005-2016. photographyicon.com/themes/.

# Index

American soldiers occupying Germany were no less souvenir hounds than their Wehrmacht counterparts. As the back of this image might attest, this soldier's neighbor in Kraiburg (roughly 45 miles east of Munich) shared this image, probably taken before or during the war, as mentioned on the reverse that the picture was "taken in their hayday [*sic*]." The sleeve length of the taller boy could be indicative of wartime clothing shortages, since supply rarely kept up with youthful growth spurts.

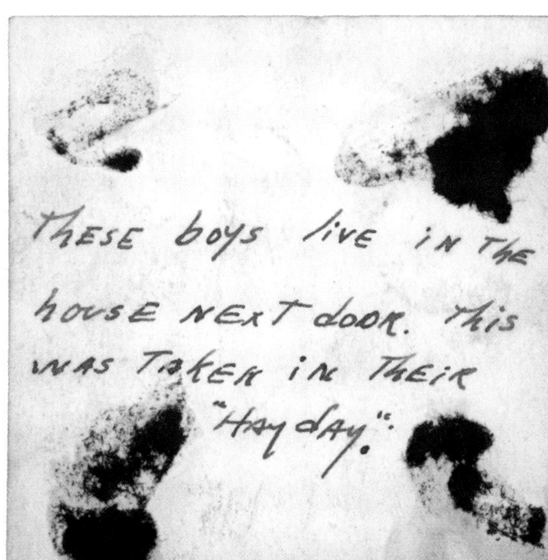

It is difficult to tell whether this woman is wearing her own uniform or that of a friend, male or female. The standard overcoat and *Schiffchen* is that of a Reichspost *Briefträger*, or letter carrier (note the satchel at her waist). One thing is clear; it appears as if she would rather be somewhere else.

Considerably more cheerful than her counterpart in the previous photo, this woman wears the same *Briefträger*'s uniform; the photo was taken either shortly before or shortly after the previous one. The fullness of the trousers and size of the boots lead one to presume the uniform is not hers.

American soldiers occupying Germany were no less souvenir hounds than their Wehrmacht counterparts. As the back of this image might attest, this soldier's neighbor in Kraiburg (roughly 45 miles east of Munich) shared this image, probably taken before or during the war, as mentioned on the reverse that the picture was "taken in their hayday [*sic*]." The sleeve length of the taller boy could be indicative of wartime clothing shortages, since supply rarely kept up with youthful growth spurts.

It is difficult to tell whether this woman is wearing her own uniform or that of a friend, male or female. The standard overcoat and *Schiffchen* is that of a Reichspost *Briefträger*, or letter carrier (note the satchel at her waist). One thing is clear; it appears as if she would rather be somewhere else.

Considerably more cheerful than her counterpart in the previous photo, this woman wears the same *Briefträger*'s uniform; the photo was taken either shortly before or shortly after the previous one. The fullness of the trousers and size of the boots lead one to presume the uniform is not hers.